fingerfood

Elsa Petersen-Schepelern

photography by William Lingwood

fingerfood

RYLAND
PETERS
& SMALL

First published in Great Britain in 1999
by Ryland Peters & Small
Cavendish House, 51–55 Mortimer Street,
London W1N 7TD

Text © Elsa Petersen-Schepelern 1999
Design and photographs
© Ryland Peters & Small 1999

Produced by Sun Fung Offset Binding Co., Ltd
Printed in China.

10 9 8 7 6 5 4 3 2 1

ISBN 1 84172 007 0

A CIP record for this book is available from the British Library.

Acknowledgements
My thanks to my sister Kirsten and my nephews Luc Votan, Zac
Stümer and Peter Bray for all their help. Thanks also to fellow
cooks, including Clare Ferguson, Rosemary Stark, Sue Holmes,
Tessa Kerwood, Susan Haynes, Ashley Western and Elle Kiss,
Michael Ryland, Fiona Smith and Sunil Vijayagar for their input,
and to 'my' author, Linda Collister, for teaching me about baking.
Particular thanks to Sheridan Lear and Maddy Bastianelli who
helped with recipe testing, to Robin Rout for his design and
William Lingwood for his beautiful photography. Thanks also to
Aero in Upper Street, Islington, for the gorgeous Mondial pocket
watch. Party people, including Mary Norden, John Herbert, Peter
Johansson, Zac and the troops from Ryland Peters & Small.
I trust that great fun was had by all.

Notes
Spoon measurements are level.
Uncooked or partly cooked eggs should not be served to the
very old or frail, the very young or to pregnant women.
Specialist Asian ingredients are available in large supermarkets,
Asian, Thai, Chinese, Japanese and Vietnamese shops.
Ⓥ Designates recipes suitable for vegetarians.

Designer
Robin Rout
Editor
Elsa Petersen-Schepelern
Assistant Editor
Maddalena Bastianelli
Production
Patricia Harrington
Head of Design
Gabriella Le Grazie
Publishing Director
Anne Ryland

Food Stylists
Sunil Vijayakar
Maddalena Bastianelli
Stylist
Mary Norden
Photographer's Assistant
Briar Pacey
Author Photograph
Francis Loney

Contents

Serve **fingerfood** that's a mixture of prepare-ahead and last-minute assemblies. You'll need 4–6 pieces per person per hour.
But above all, choose recipes that will help to take the panic out of partying!

What kind of party?

The recipes in this book are designed to be served as finger food at a drinks party. Usually such parties last for 2–3 hours. If you've asked people for a longer time, then you should also serve them one or more substantial dishes.

You can also use the recipes as nibbles to serve with drinks before a dinner party – just choose your dishes well, so you don't fill people up before dinner, or clash with the courses you're serving for dinner. Take care with quantities too – many's the time I've had to wrest the Flat Beans with Hoummus from people who've come to dinner, in case they didn't have any room left for the main event.

How many people?

The size of your party will depend on the size of your house – or garden – and the capacity of your kitchen. In a small flat, half a dozen people might be the limit. In a larger house or a garden, the numbers might swell to dozens, or even hundreds (though if you've invited hundreds, I suggest you call in the professionals!).

Recipe choice

Choose 4–6 items per hour – several easy things from the first chapter, then one each from other chapters.

Sweet things, like ice cream and cake should be served towards the end of the party – they signal 'finale'.

Unless you have a large house, where cooking smells won't invade the party, cook deep-fried items the morning or day before, then reheat in the oven.

Recipe order

Serve treats like oysters, prawns or caviar first, with proper fanfare.

In fact, treat your party menu like an ordinary meal. Serve light and fresh things first, such as soups or morsels wrapped in leaves, then more substantial foods like sushi, hamburgers or bruschetta – to help soak up the alcohol. Follow these with rice, bread or pastry, then the more substantial dishes of meat or poultry.

Then something light and salady, then savoury and cheesy, then sweet. Most people can't drink any more alcohol after sweet things.

One Thing at a Time

Serve just one kind of food at a time. Remember those who don't eat meat, or can't eat the kind you're offering. So include a vegetarian or chicken option. These recipes are marked Ⓥ beside the serving quantity for each recipe.

Waiters and Sous Chefs

Depending on the size of your party, it's only sensible to have helpers – family or friends, professional waiters or chefs.

Hire them far in advance, and brief them well before they start serving. They must know what to do, how you want them to do it, and what they're serving.

Food Facts

How much food?

It depends how long your party will be, and how many cooks will be available to prepare the food.

I think that one cook – that's you – can cope with about 8 different dishes, but only if you are able to prepare at least half of them in advance. If you plan to serve more, you'll need help – either from family and friends, or hired from an agency. Prepare each dish on the assembly-line principle, completing one task before beginning the next.

Serve 4–6 items each hour per guest, so for 30 people for 2 hours you need 8–12 different dishes – that's at least 240 items, so plan ahead.

What kind of food?

The best collections of finger foods include a range of textures and flavours to please the guests, and several different preparation and cooking methods to make life easier for the cook. Include:

- Crunchy things, like crisps, chips, deep-fried spring rolls or wontons.

- Savoury, salty things like Anchovy Pinwheels and Spiced Nuts.

- Substantial things to soak up the alcohol, like mini hamburgers and hot dogs, pizza and bruschetta.

- Creamy things like Leaves with Hoummus and Tabbouleh Salad, Mini Bagels or Blini with Cream Cheese and Smoked Salmon.

- Sweet Things (optional) as a final treat, particularly if it's a special occasion like Christmas or a birthday.

Special dietary requirements

Remember some of your guests may have special requirements. Mostly, they will organize for themselves which of your dishes they would like to or can eat. But think of them when you're planning your menu.

- If they're weight-watchers, have pity. Don't make every single thing deep-fried or creamy.

- If some have religious taboos, don't serve too many dishes made with pork, seafood or beef.

- Some may be vegetarian, so make sure there are several things they can eat (and make sure your waiters know which they are). Vegetarian dishes in this book have been marked with a special symbol after the serving quantity – Ⓥ.

- Some guests may even be vegan – that means no animal products of any kind, including eggs, cheese or cream. Point them toward vegetable sushi or stuffed vine leaves, and have some bruschetta that will suit them.

- Some people have allergies, for instance to peanuts, strawberries, chillies or prawns. Most allergic people are alert for foods which may cause problems, but if you know your friends have allergies like these, either leave out that ingredient or make sure your waiters know which foods contain the problem element.

Drips

Finger food should be confined to things that can be eaten in one bite – or two at most.

Above all, it must not be unwieldy – the kind of food that tumbles or drips down people's shirtfronts.

Your guests should be able to hold a drink in one hand and the food in the other. Or perhaps both items in one hand, leaving the other free for talking.

Forward preparation

If you're making many different bite-sized foods, you must plan ahead. Prepare some dishes in advance, freezing some, chilling others and storing yet others in airtight containers for 1 or 2 days.

Have your oven preheated for about 15 minutes before the party starts so you can reheat some ready-prepared dishes and give a quick final cooking to others. I set mine at 200°C (400°F) Gas 6 throughout the party.

I also have a collection of electronic timers which beep madly as each item is ready. Then you won't miscalculate and burn the food.

Food safety

When you have a party, you're catering for large numbers of people and storing larger quantities of food than usual.

Remember to keep food preparation areas, utensils and hands scrupulously clean. Before and after cooking, heat and cool foods quickly, so they spend as little time as possible in the danger zone for microbe-multiplication. Do not put hot or warm food in the refrigerator, which should remain below 4°C and above 1°C.

Dry or salty items, such as nuts, crisps, caperberries or olives are safe, because microbes don't flourish under these conditions.

When you reheat, do so thoroughly (without burning the food to a crisp). It should be kept at 63°C or hotter until ready to serve. However, when you serve the food, don't serve it blisteringly hot, or people will burn themselves.

How much food can you fit in your own fridge and freezer? When you're catering for lots of people, you won't necessarily have room for it all. That means you must borrow other people's fridges and freezers – or even hire them.

10 Party Drinks

How much?

Better too much than too little. Be generous! Most suppliers will let you return what you don't use, so it's always better to allow a little more.

Some people will drink – others won't. And you may not know until they get there! Just remember to have enough for both kinds of guests.

Champagne

My favourite party drink is champagne. For a 2-hour party, allow about ½ bottle per guest, for a 3-hour party, ¾ bottle for each person. That looks after the people who drink more and those who drink nothing at all.

There are 6 glasses in a bottle – or 8 if you're mixing it to make Kir (page 134) or a Champagne Cocktail (page 139).

Serve a light, dry kind – such as Mumm, Cuvée Napa, a cava or Green Point – it doesn't have to be French.

Wine

Again, about ½ bottle per person. When serving wine, you'll probably find people prefer white, with a few die-hards who don't drink anything but red.

Make sure it's good quality and not so distinctive that people's palates will pall after 2 hours of it.

The ratio of white to red will be different in summer and winter. In summer, allow 3 bottles of white wine to 1 of red, and in winter, make them equal – but you know your own guests.

But let's face it, if you allow 1 bottle per person, you can always serve the leftovers at your next dinner party.

Cocktails

Cocktails are a stylish choice, but limit yourself to 2–3 different kinds – one from the brandy-whisky family, then another from the gin-vodka group and one from the hold-onto-your-hat gang; tequila, rum, etc.

If you don't have barmen on hand, and since it's difficult to prepare cocktails in advance, choose something easy to make. Cocktails can be pretty intoxicating, so many people like to have just one, or possibly two, then move onto another kind of party drink.

Garnishes

Order lots of limes and lemons, and cut them into slices and wedges in advance, and cover with clingfilm to stop them drying out.

Other garnishes will depend on the drinks you're serving. Olives and lemon zest for Martinis, maraschino cherries for Manhattans, cucumber for Pimms. And mint for Juleps of course.

Spirits

If a person is a Scotch drinker, he (and he's often a he) won't be fobbed off with wine. There are 16 measures in a 750 ml bottle of Scotch and other spirits. Three is all most people will manage in a 2-hour party.

It's not necessary to offer every spirit available – the three most popular, Scotch, vodka and gin, are probably enough, though tequila and bourbon also have their dedicated followers.

Mixers

Mixers should include sparkling and still mineral water, soda water, cola, tonic, dry ginger, orange, grapefruit and tomato juice.

Punch-bowl drinks

Big party drinks which can, mercifully, be prepared or part-prepared, in advance include Planter's Punch, Sangria, non-alcoholic punch, Glögg or glühwein, and so on.

The very strong ones, like Planter's Punch, contain about the same amount of alcohol as a strong measure of spirits, so cater accordingly.

The lighter, wine-based drinks such as Sangria contain only a little less alcohol than wine itself, so cater as for wine.

Mineral water and soft drinks

Allow 1 bottle for every 3 or 4 people, and divide the quantity between still and sparkling water.

The Designated Drivers and other teetotallers will be delighted if you make an effort with their drinks, and even the drinkers will be glad of something fresh when they decide to stop drinking.

Remember – lots of ice!

Serving
Ideas

Because finger food is usually an assembly of many small things, how you present them is important. The more attractive the presentation, the more delicious the food will appear.

Throughout this book, I've given you lots of ideas about presentation.

Bite-size containers

Sometimes I have suggested you use bite-sized containers, such as:

- spoons
- paper cones
- waxpaper cups
- shot glasses
- demitasse coffee cups
- Moroccan tea glasses
- cocktail sticks and toothpicks
- satay sticks and chopsticks.

Foods like crisps and nuts will not only taste better in separate containers, but serving them in little twists and cones are more hygienic too.

Serving trays

You will already have a collection of serving trays in your kitchen, so dress them up in lots of ways, with napkins, leaves, linens and papers.

But be careful – make sure they won't be too heavy to carry, because when they're loaded with food, they're going to be even heavier!

However, though everyone has a collection of plates and trays, they don't usually have enough for a party. So – hire them, borrow them, or improvize, as we have here.

Improvised trays can be made from:

- cane baskets and plates
- wooden chopping boards
- tennis rackets and pingpong bats
- oven racks and cake cooling trays
- cardboard and wooden boxes and their shallow lids (keep any glamorous chocolate boxes any one gives you – they make perfect serving trays)
- bark tubs and even flower pots
- heavy card, folded into box shapes and secured with cocktail sticks.

Tray cloths

Cover trays with:

- tracing paper
- blotting paper
- folded brown paper
- coloured gift papers, but take care that the dyes won't harm the food
- fresh and dried leaves
- tray cloths and table napkins
- linens and hessians, hemmed, torn or scissor-cut.

Your imagination is the only limit!

Countdown

One week ahead

• Order drinks, glasses, ice, ice buckets and bins for ice, drinks and rubbish. Most suppliers will let you return any bottles you don't use, and will hire much of the equipment you need.

• Assemble all your serving trays and buy or make others if required.

• Assemble special serving items, such as paper twists and cones, cocktail napkins, tray cloths, tablecloths, baskets, cocktail sticks and bamboo skewers.

• Arrange candles and music.

• Organize kitchen equipment required for the menu you've chosen.

• Prepare dishes to be frozen and cooked from frozen or thawed and reheated.

Two to three days ahead

• Prepare those items that can be prepared then kept in an airtight container until just before serving.

• Make ice creams, wrap Christmas cake logs in icing, buy ready-rolled pastry.

• Write final shopping lists, ordering from suppliers where necessary.

One day ahead

• Buy all the food, except the most perishable, such as oysters and prawns. I prefer to buy salad leaves and herbs the day I want to use them.

• Prepare meats, sauces and marinades. Marinate meats for skewer recipes and chill overnight, either before or after threading onto wooden skewers (skewers should stay damp until ready to cook).

• Cook recipes such as rare roast beef which can be chilled overnight.

• Prepare basic mixtures for macerated drinks such as Glögg or punch.

• Arrange the room and prepare the bar area, set out glasses, cocktail sticks, napkins, any cocktail equipment and (many) corkscrews, champagne cork claws and other equipment.

• Check drinks are cold. (Chilling large quantities of drinks at the last minute is asking for trouble!)

• Check straws, linen and napkins.

Morning of party

• Collect foods such as salad leaves, herbs, creams etc.

• Prepare remaining dressings and salsas (page 36) and any herbs or garnishes (float herb sprigs in a bowl of iced water and cover with clingfilm).

• Cut up any vegetables needed for recipes and cover with clingfilm.

• Assemble dishes that are able to stand, such as quails' eggs.

Afternoon of party

• Assemble and cook all dishes except those that require last-minute preparation and cooking.

Two hours ahead

• Begin cooking and assembling food, and assemble dishes such as pizzas that need last-minute cooking.

One hour ahead

• Prepare recipes such as Danish Open Sandwiches. Spread with butter, cut and chill ready for topping.

Thirty minutes ahead

• Preheat the oven.

• Party should be ready to go and first dishes ready to serve. Draw corks from still wines. Prepare the materials for cocktails. Sit down!

When the first guest arrives

• Pull the champagne corks and take the coats. Serve cocktails and champagne.

13

Who said party food had to be difficult and complicated? This chapter, **spoons, cups and quickies**, shows that simple but delicious ingredients, simply served, can taste wonderful and look spectacular. And they make life easier for the cook.

Smoked Salmon Brochettes

Who said party food had to be difficult and complicated? This simple idea can be prepared in the morning, covered with clingfilm and refrigerated until just before serving (it will taste better if you let it come back to room temperature first).

250 g smoked salmon

finely grated zest of 2 lemons

freshly cracked black pepper

Serves 12

Cut slices of smoked salmon lengthways into long strips, about 1 cm wide and 10 cm long. Most slices will produce about 3 strips.) Thread the strips carefully onto cocktail sticks.

Arrange the loaded sticks on a serving platter and sprinkle with finely grated lemon zest and cracked black pepper.

Ice-cold Prairie Oysters

Prairie Oysters are usually regarded as a hangover cure – but take away their medicinal nature, and replace the egg yolk with a real oyster, and they are utterly delicious! Serve this as a one-off canapé-cum-cocktail when people first arrive. Make sure all the ingredients are ice-cold, and the vodka has been in the freezer.

600 ml tomato juice

200 ml ice-cold vodka

juice of 6 limes or 2 large lemons

a dash of Tabasco, or to taste

crushed ice

12 freshly shucked oysters

salt and freshly ground black pepper

sprigs of fresh mint (optional)

mini wedges or slivers of lime, to serve

Serves 12

Put the tomato juice, vodka, lime or lemon juice and Tabasco in a jug half-full of crushed ice. Stir well. (If making in advance, omit the ice and chill well.)

Put 1 oyster in each of 12 shot glasses, aquavit or sherry glasses, add the chilled vodka mixture, then top with a mint leaf or lime zest, a little salt and pepper and a lime wedge speared with a cocktail stick. Use any leftover Bloody Mary mixture for people who don't like oysters.

Variation: Before you start, rub a lemon wedge around the rim of each glass, and press the rim into a saucer of salt, just as if you were making a Margarita.

Ever since I saw this idea in a food magazine, I've served many different things in **spoons**, from caviar to ice cream. It always looks just fabulous.

Spoonfuls of Caviar

A spoonful of caviar is incredibly luxurious and a rare treat for most of us. Serve it early in the party, perhaps first-off, with a shot glass of ice-cold vodka. Champagne or white wine is also a good choice!

Unless you're very rich, confine this spectacular dish to very small gatherings! One 50 g can of caviar will serve 8 people. Beluga is sold in a blue can, followed by Oscietre in yellow and Sevruga in red. Though Beluga is the most highly regarded, the slightly less expensive Sevruga is probably better for a party.

Remember – never serve caviar in a metal spoon. Use bone, wood, glass – even plastic.

50 g can of caviar or salmon keta

Serves about 8

Using a plastic teaspoon, carefully take one spoonful out of the can, without breaking any of the eggs.

Put into a serving teaspoon, smoothing it carefully (remember – no metal!).

Repeat until you have enough for each guest. Arrange the spoons on a plate (rectangular is better) and serve.

Variation: Other kinds of caviar are also delicious. Try Salmon Keta, Trout Eggs, Tuna Eggs, Lumpfish, Mullet, Sea Urchin or American Caviar.

For larger gatherings, other dishes can be served on spoons – or try them in leaves (pages 78–81).

Spoonfuls of Goats' Cheese ⓥ

In a small bowl, mix 250 g goats' cheese, 125 ml cream, 1 bunch of chives, scissor-snipped, salt and freshly ground black pepper.

Using a melon baller or the smallest ice cream scoop dipped into boiling water, scoop out balls of the mixture and place in a teaspoon or Chinese porcelain soup spoon. Arrange the spoons on a platter and serve.

Spoonfuls of Spicy Thai Salad

Mix 2 teaspoons fresh lime juice in a bowl with 2 teaspoons fish sauce or soy sauce, 1 teaspoon sugar and 2 chopped red chillies. Mix until the sugar dissolves, then stir in 500 g cooked crabmeat. Serve as above.

Spoonfuls of Keta, Gravlax and Chives

Mix 250 g gravlax, finely chopped, with 4 tablespoons scissor-snipped fresh chives. Put spoonfuls on the serving spoons, flatten slightly, then top with a small pile of keta (salmon caviar) or flying fish roe. A little crème fraîche or sour cream between the layers is also delicious.

19

Gazpacho

An unusual gazpacho with clear, bright tastes. Make sure all the vegetables are ice-cold.

4 yellow or orange peppers

1 punnet yellow cherry tomatoes, halved, plus 12 red cherry tomatoes, quartered, to serve

2 garlic cloves, crushed with salt

3 mini cucumbers

6 radishes

6 spring onions, white and green, sliced

1 bunch of chives, snipped (optional)

tiny sprigs of mint or basil

salt and cracked black pepper, to taste

Serves 24 Ⓥ

Peel the peppers with a vegetable peeler, then core and chop the flesh into a blender. Add the yellow tomatoes, garlic and 750 ml crushed ice and blend to a vibrant yellow purée. Chill until ready to serve.

Cut the cucumbers in half lengthways and scrape out and discard the seeds. Thinly slice the cucumbers and radishes diagonally on a mandoline. Slice the spring onions diagonally crossways.

Put the purée (thinned a little with water if necessary) into small cups, glasses or waxpaper cups, add pieces of cucumber, radish, red cherry tomato and spring onion. Sprinkle with the herbs, sea salt and cracked black pepper, then serve.

Pea Soup with Mint

Freshly shelled peas are best – you can cheat with frozen ones, but cook them for a shorter time. For the harassed party host, I give a microwave-blender version.

1 tablespoon olive oil

8 slices pancetta

600 g shelled fresh peas

1 litre boiling chicken stock

sea salt and freshly ground black pepper

mint tips, to serve

Serves 24

Heat the olive oil in a pan, add the pancetta and fry until crispy. Remove and drain on crumpled kitchen paper.

Microwave the peas on HIGH for about 4 minutes or until tender. Transfer to a blender, add 250 ml stock, salt and pepper. Zap to a purée, then add the remaining stock and blend again. Taste and adjust the seasoning, then add extra stock or boiling water if too thick.

Pour into waxpaper cups, demitasse coffee cups or heatproof glasses. Serve, topped with crispy pancetta and mint tips.

Note: The soup will thicken as it cools, so make it a little thinner than you want the end result to be.

Sweet Potato Soup

A delicious tropical soup using orange sweet potatoes – use pumpkin instead if you like.

1 onion, finely chopped

2 garlic cloves, crushed

3 cm fresh ginger, grated

2 stalks lemongrass, finely chopped

2 red chillies or 1 tablespoon red Thai curry paste

1 tablespoon lime juice

3 tablespoons peanut oil

500 g sweet potatoes (about 2 large)

500 ml canned coconut milk

500 ml vegetable or chicken stock

salt and freshly ground black pepper

To serve:

finely grated kaffir lime zest

finely sliced red chillies

Serves 24 Ⓥ

Put the onion, garlic, ginger, lemongrass, chillies or curry paste, lime juice and 2 tablespoons of the peanut oil in a blender or spice grinder and zap until smooth.

Heat a wok, then swirl in the remaining oil. Add the spice paste and cook gently for 5 minutes. Do not let it burn.

Add the sweet potatoes, coconut milk and stock. Simmer, uncovered, until the sweet potatoes are soft. Transfer to the blender and zap again. Season to taste, reheat if necessary and serve in waxpaper or demitasse cups or heatproof glasses, topped with finely grated kaffir lime zest and sliced red chilli.

These **quick assemblies**, are so simple that they don't need much in the way of a recipe, just a few serving ideas.

These dishes are invaluable as finger food, because one or more of them can be prepared earlier, covered to keep them moist, then brought out between your more time-consuming efforts.

Oysters on Ice

There is nothing better than a plate of super-fresh chilled oysters still in their liquor.

Arrange them on a plate of sea salt and seaweed, and prepare them properly without any specks of shell, and with the oyster properly detached from the shell. Add lemon wedges (though I think oysters are better absolutely plain).

Serve with chilled champagne or white wine, but never ever with whisky!

Quails' Eggs with Dipping Spice

Quails' eggs are just incredibly pretty – but quite difficult to peel. You have to pierce the shell, then the very tough membrane under the shell. If unavailable, use small hens' eggs, halved, instead.

1 dozen quails' eggs

2 tablespoons celery salt, salt mixed with pepper or dried crushed chillies, Japanese seven-spice, furikake seasoning or a dip of your choice (pages 36–37)

Serves 12 Ⓥ

Put the quails' eggs into a small saucepan of cold water and bring to the boil. Simmer for 3 minutes, then turn off the heat, drain immediately and fill the pan with cold water.

Tap the shells all over, then peel under running water. Arrange on a small serving plate, with a dish of celery salt, spiced salt, furikake seasoning or a dip.

I like to put one or two back into a small base of shell because the shells are so pretty. Try not to include any unshelled eggs, because there's always someone who's not seen them before and will try to eat the whole egg, shell and all!

Variation: Shell all the eggs and serve in a basket, half-and-half with fat black olives.

Char-grilled Indian Cheese

Other cheeses, such as Greek haloumi or Italian provolone, can be used for this dish, but the original uses Indian paneer cheese. The recipe is a favourite from my friend Usha, a great cook, who lives in Agra, the city of the Taj Mahal.

peanut or mustard oil or ghee, for brushing

500 g paneer*, haloumi or provolone cheese, cut into 2 cm cubes

Makes about 8 Ⓥ

Brush a stove-top grill pan with oil or ghee. Briefly char-grill or pan-fry the cubes of cheese until lightly browned on all sides. Serve warm or cool.

*Note: Paneer is sold in Asian markets and some supermarkets. To make it yourself, put 1 litre whole milk in a saucepan, bring to the boil, stir in 2 tablespoons fresh lemon juice and 2 tablespoons plain yoghurt. When the milk curdles, pour it into a colander or strainer lined with muslin and let drain for 3 hours. Cover with muslin, put a plate on top and a heavy food can on top of that. Chill for 4 hours or overnight until the cheese hardens a little (the longer you leave it, the harder it will be), then turn out and cut into cubes. Let drain on a clean cloth, then use as above.

Flat Beans and Hoummus

This dish is so simple – and incredibly popular. I have served this with drinks before dinner parties and people have loved it so much they've almost had no room for the rest of the food!

500 g flat beans or runner beans

250 ml hoummus, either store-bought or home-made

To serve (optional):

2 teaspoons extra-virgin olive oil

freshly cracked black pepper

Serves 6–8 (V)

Top and tail the beans, then cut them diagonally into 3–5 cm sections.

Spoon the hoummus into a small bowl and swirl the top. Sprinkle with olive oil and pepper, if using.

Put the bowl on a serving platter with the beans beside.

Prawns

make superb finger food. Medium-sized ones, peeled and deveined, with just the tail fin intact to act as a handle, might have been specially designed for the purpose.

The golden rule is to make sure the prawns are sparkling fresh and taste marvellous. If you're buying ready-cooked prawns, you can taste one first to make sure they're good. If you're cooking your own, you are at the mercy of the handling methods. But the way you cook them can help too. Just plunge them into salted boiling water and remove as soon as they turn opaque. Cool them quickly over ice. (Overcooking will ruin them in an instant.) Don't go washing and rinsing them all the time, either, or you'll rinse away all the flavour.

Plunged Shrimp with Chilli Mojo

An easy recipe with one simple requirement – perfect prawns. Test before you buy: texture is all, they must be firm, with tightly curled tails.

1–3 cooked or uncooked prawns per person, depending on size

Chilli Mojo (page 37)

Serves 1

If using uncooked prawns, insert a cocktail stick at the neck of each prawn and pull out the dark vein.

Bring a large pan of well salted water to the boil (you can also add a sheet of kombu seaweed, removing it just before boiling point). Plunge in the prawns and cook just until the flesh is opaque (about 3 minutes, depending on the size of the prawns).

Remove with a wire basket or slotted spoon and plunge immediately into a large bowl of iced water to stop the cooking (don't leave them there too long, or you'll wash away the flavour). Remove and chill over ice.

Cut off the heads and remove the shells and legs, but leave the tail fins intact (keep the heads and shells in the freezer and use to make bisques or other seafood soups).

Put the prawns on a plate or tray with a bowl of Chilli Mojo and serve.

Great Caribbean vegetables make superb **crisps**. Make them with one or all of the following fruit and vegetables.

My absolute favourite is plantain, the cooking banana just packed with fibre (if you can't find plantains, use green bananas). Cook as many crisps as possible, because they're eaten almost as fast as you can make them. You can cook these early in the day and keep them in an airtight container until ready to serve (they will keep for up to 3 days, but seem to lose a little crispness each day). Always try to use a good-quality oil such as peanut, sunflower or corn oil – those labelled as vegetable oil often have a mix of oils, some very cheap and often over-refined.

Plantain Crisps

6 plantains, green if possible, or yellow, but not black, or 12 green bananas

sunflower oil, for frying

To serve, your choice of:

mild chilli powder

chilli dipping sauce

Serves about 20 Ⓥ

To peel the plantains, cut off the points at either end, then run the tip of your knife down the length of the fruit, just piercing the skin. Do this in 3–4 places. Carefully run your thumbs under the skin, easing it off. (Another way is to soak the slit plantains in warm water for 10 minutes before peeling.)

Using a vegetable peeler or mandoline, cut long lengthways strips off the plantain. To make thicker crisps, as shown, cut diagonally with a knife.

Meanwhile, fill a wok one-third full of oil and heat to 190°C (375°F). (I prefer a wok because you're not wasting lots of extra oil in the corners.) Alternatively, fill a deep-fat-fryer with oil and heat to the recommended temperature.

Add the plantain strips in batches and fry until crisp and golden. Remove with a slotted spoon and drain on crumpled kitchen paper.

When all the crisps are cooked, serve immediately, or let cool and transfer to an airtight container until ready to use.

To serve, sprinkle sparingly with chilli powder (don't make it too hot – some people won't like it) and serve in twists or cones of paper.

Alternatively, place on a serving platter with a dish of chilli dipping sauce.

Caribbean Crisps

Wonderful crisps can be made with other starchy vegetables such as sweet potatoes, pumpkin, yams or parsnips.

Your choice of:

about 500 g white or orange sweet potatoes (shown)

about 500 g yams, such as eddoes, yellow, coco or Ghana yam

about 500 g pumpkin, deseeded but not peeled

about 500 g parsnips

sunflower oil, for frying

spices such as cumin, mixed spice or Thai 7-spice, to serve

Serves about 20 Ⓥ

Finely slice the vegetables on a mandoline, cutting them into narrower strips if necessary.

Fry and drain on crumpled kitchen paper as in the previous recipe, then sprinkle with spices and serve.

Variation:

Aubergine Crisps Ⓥ

Deep-fry finely sliced aubergines (shown left) as in the previous recipe, but at 180°C (350°F) for 10 minutes, taking care they don't burn. Don't cook too quickly, or the chips will drink up too much oil. Remove with a slotted spoon and drain on crumpled kitchen paper, as in the previous recipe. If not crisp, increase the heat to 190°C (375°F) and fry for 30 seconds longer. Drain again and serve sprinkled with sea salt flakes.

Oven-baked Tomatoes

I think sun-dried tomatoes are rather leathery in texture and overwhelming in flavour, except when used to make pesto. However, if you oven-roast fresh tomatoes until they've collapsed, they are wonderful as toppings for bruschetta and pizzas.
If you keep roasting them until they're half-dry, they make a delicious if less crunchy addition to the crisp repertoire.

12 small tomatoes (the next size up from cherries) or mini plum tomatoes

sugar

sea salt

2–3 garlic cloves, cut into fine slivers (optional)

Makes 24 Ⓥ

Cut the tomatoes in half crossways and cut out the dense central core with a small sharp knife. Arrange apart on oven trays. Top each half with a pinch of sugar and a few flakes of sea salt. Push 2 fine slivers of garlic, if using, into the seed section of each tomato half.

Roast in a preheated oven at 200°C (400°F) Gas 6 for about 1 hour. Test after 30 minutes and 45 minutes. When collapsed, browned, but still soft they can be used as a topping for pizzas and bruschetta, or served as a vegetable.

Cook for about 15 minutes longer and they will have dried out enough to be served as a nibble, as shown.

Everyone loves traditional **fish and chips** turned into a mini serving for a party and everyone cheers up considerably.

The secret to making perfect chips is to twice-fry them. This is just as important for these super-fine chips cut on a mandoline. If you don't have a mandoline, cut them very finely into matchstick lengths.

6 large potatoes, cut into matchsticks

500 g salmon fillet, sliced in half lengthways, then crossways into 1 cm wide strips

sunflower, corn or peanut oil, for frying

Tempura batter:

40 g cornflour

40 g plain flour

1 teaspoon baking powder

5 teaspoons sunflower, corn or peanut oil

175 ml soda water or beer

Serves 20

Assemble all the ingredients for the tempura batter, but do not mix it.

Fill a wok one-third full of oil and heat to 190°C (375°F). Alternatively, fill a deep-fryer with oil and heat to the recommended temperature.

Add the potato strips in batches and fry for about 2 minutes until creamy coloured. Remove with a slotted spoon and spread out to drain on crumpled kitchen paper. When all the chips are fried, reheat the oil and fry them again until crisp and golden. Drain on crumpled kitchen paper and keep them warm in the oven. They should be so crisp they rustle together.

Skim the oil and reheat to 190°C (375°F).

Put a large bowl to the left of the wok (if you're right-handed) and a serving platter lined with crumpled kitchen paper to the right. Have the fish to the left of the bowl. Put the batter ingredients into the bowl and mix quickly with chopsticks, leaving as lumpy as possible, and with a rim of flour left unmixed around the bowl.

Using a pair of long chopsticks or tongs, dip each piece of fish quickly into the batter then place gently in the hot oil. Fry until golden, then remove and drain on crumpled kitchen paper.

To serve, put a pinch of the potato chips into each container (in this case a twist of newspaper lined with greaseproof paper) and add a piece of tempura fish. Make sure all the ingredients are lined up vertically, so people don't drop any on the floor.

Serve immediately. You may need to reheat these a little – put them in the oven, in the paper cones and heat with the oven door open for a few minutes. No longer or they will get too hot (and the paper may burn).

Yes, I know you can buy **roasted nuts**, but it's easy to roast your own, and you can add all sorts of delicious spices to them to make them more personal.

34

They look wonderful, too, served in tiny individual cones, dishes or boxes. People can hold a drink and a cone in one hand and pick out the nuts with the other. It avoids all those anxieties about many hands dipping into the bowl of nuts.

The quantities will vary according to the number of people you have, what else you're serving, how hungry they were to start with and when in the party you serve them. I think the crisps and nuts come early in the party, right after the first drink.

Serve 1–3 kinds of nuts, but serve each kind separately. I think I would break my golden rule of only one kind of food on the plate too, if people can't tell the difference between a peanut and an almond, they're already having a thoroughly good time and won't care.

your choice of freshly ground or crushed spices, such as:

cinnamon sticks

cardamom

nutmeg

mild chilli flakes

sesame seeds

cumin seeds

paprika

ginger

black pepper

grated citrus zest

Thai 7-spice

Japanese 7-spice

your choice of fresh, raw nuts, about 30 g or 2 tablespoons per person, such as:

peanuts

cashews

macadamias

almonds

pecans

1 tablespoon sunflower oil, for toasting (optional)

sea salt flakes

Serves 8 Ⓥ

The number one rule is – fresh nuts and freshly ground spices. Break up the cinnamon sticks and grind them to a powder in a coffee grinder or with a mortar and pestle.

Wipe out the grinder, then grind the black seeds from the green cardamom pods (or buy them already podded – if you do it yourself, the seeds can be a little sticky). If using nutmeg, grate whole ones with a nutmeg grater, or on the finest side of a box grater.

To roast the nuts, heat a dry frying pan, add one kind of nut and cook, shaking the pan, until they're aromatic and slightly golden. You must stay with them, and keep shaking, or they will burn and be spoiled.

When ready, tip them into a wide, shallow bowl, then sprinkle with salt and one of the spices or citrus zest.

If preferred, you can cook the nuts with 1 tablespoon of sunflower oil, but your guests will love the flavour of dry-fried nuts and thank you for saving them from that tiny extra drop of oil.

To serve, drop about 2 tablespoons of the nuts into each paper twist, tiny china bowl or folded mini box, arrange in a basket and serve.

Like many of the recipes in this book, **dips** are mix-and-match with other recipes.

Mexican Salsa is good as a dipping sauce, on bruschetta or mixed with chicken and served in baby lettuce leaves.

1 large red chilli, halved

1 mango, deseeded and chopped

½ papaya, deseeded and chopped

1 small red onion, finely diced

juice of 2 limes

juice of 1 orange

2 garlic cloves, crushed

2 teaspoons caster sugar

a pinch of salt

Makes about 500 ml Ⓥ

Grill the chilli until the skin is blistered (not too long, or the flesh will become bitter). Remove, then scrape off and discard the burnt skin and all the membranes. Chop the flesh.

Put all the ingredients in a bowl and stir well. Mash a little with a fork if necessary.

Aubergine purée – **Baba Ganoush** – is one of the greatest dishes from the Middle East, and variations are found everywhere from Poland to Perth.

1 large aubergine

2 fat garlic cloves, crushed

125 ml tahini paste

125 ml lemon juice

salt

1 small bunch parsley, finely chopped

Makes about 500 ml Ⓥ

Prick the aubergine all over with a fork. Cook in a preheated oven at about 200°C (400°F) Gas 6 for about 30 minutes*, or until the outside is charred and the inside is soft and fluffy. (Some traditional recipes suggest that the aubergine be charred over an open flame, or under a grill, but I was taught by a splendid Polish cook, who just put it in the oven.)

Peel off and discard the charred skin, rinsing off any remaining black bits with water. Put the peeled flesh into a food processor with the garlic, tahini, lemon juice and salt. Pulse to a purée, taste and adjust the seasoning, then transfer to a serving bowl. Sprinkle with parsley and serve warm or at room temperature. The purée may be covered and refrigerated overnight, but return to room temperature before using. Serve as a dip, on top of pizzas (page 50), with pitta bread (page 96), or stuffed into ciabatta pockets (page 84) either alone or with lamb.

*Note: The time will depend on the size and shape of the eggplant. Keep testing.

Variation: Omit the tahini paste and this purée becomes aubergine pesto.

A **Satay Sauce** contains peanuts, so you might like to serve a plain soy sauce dip as well in case some people can't have nuts.

125 ml fresh peanuts or peanut butter

5 dried red chillies

8 small shallots or 1 large mild onion

1 garlic clove, crushed

4 candlenuts or 8 almonds

1 stalk lemongrass, finely chopped, or lemon juice

2 tablespoons peanut oil

250 ml coconut milk

2 teaspoons tamarind paste or lime juice

1 teaspoon brown sugar

salt

Makes about 500 ml Ⓥ

Put the fresh peanuts, if using, in a dry frying pan and toast until brown but not burned. Crush coarsely.

Soak the dried chillies in boiling water to cover for about 30 minutes. Transfer to a spice grinder or blender, add the shallots or onion, garlic, candlenuts or almonds and lemongrass or lemon juice and work to a paste.

Heat the oil in a wok or frying pan, add the chilli mixture and sauté gently for about 5 minutes, stirring several times. Add the coconut milk and simmer, stirring constantly (keep stirring, and don't cover the pan, or the coconut milk will curdle). Add the tamarind paste or lime juice, sugar, salt and peanuts or peanut butter. Simmer for about 2 minutes, cool a little and serve.

Note: If this sauce sits for any length of time, you may need to thin it a little with hot water before serving.

Spanish and Mexican Chilli **Mojos** are a little more liquid than a salsa.

Vietnamese Nuóc Cham is a delicious, piquant, salty, spicy condiment used as an all-purpose dipping sauce. Serve it with deep-fried morsels like spring rolls (page 112), wontons (page 114), or dumplings, fresh spring rolls (page 90) or dim sum—or any number of everyday dishes.

Rouille, the Mediterranean mayonnaise-style sauce, is perfect with seafood. **Aioli** is made in the same way, omitting the chillies and bread from the recipe below.

4 tablespoons chopped fresh flat leaf parsley

1 tablespoon chopped oregano or marjoram

a pinch of salt

a pinch of sugar

3 garlic cloves, crushed

grated zest of 1 lime

125 ml freshly squeezed lime juice

1 large red chilli, cored, deseeded and finely chopped, plus 1 small red chilli, sliced (optional)

Makes about 250 ml Ⓥ

Put the herbs, salt, sugar, garlic, lime zest and lime juice in a blender and work until smooth. Taste and add more sugar if necessary. Transfer to a serving dish and stir in the chopped chilli.

Taste again, and add the extra sliced chilli, if using. Chill for 30 minutes to 3 hours to develop the flavours.

2 garlic cloves, crushed

1 red chilli, cored and chopped

1 tablespoon caster sugar

½ lime, quartered, deseeded and chopped

1½ tablespoons fish sauce

Makes about 250 ml

Work the garlic, chilli and sugar to a purée in a spice grinder or mortar and pestle. Add the chopped lime and any collected juice and purée again. Stir in the fish sauce and about 125 ml water, then serve in small dipping bowls.

3 garlic cloves, crushed

2 large fresh red chillies (or dried chillies, soaked for 15 minutes in hot water), deseeded and finely chopped

1 thick slice fresh bread, dipped in water, then squeezed dry

salt

2 egg yolks

1 egg

about 75–125 ml olive oil

Makes about 250 ml Ⓥ

Put the garlic, chillies, bread, salt, egg yolks and egg in a blender or small food processor and work to a paste. Gradually add the oil, drop by drop at first, then more quickly, to produce a thick creamy sauce.

Potatoes and other **vegetables**, make wonderful party food – filling and delicious and a treat for everyone, not just vegetarians.

Baby Potatoes

If you can find blue or yellow-fleshed potatoes, use them for this dish – the effect is spectacular.

500 g baby potatoes such as creamy Anya, Pink Fir Apple or Purple Congo

Toppings:

sour cream and caviar or salmon keta

goats' cheese and chives

cream cheese and chillies

avocado and bacon

mango chutney or pickle

red or green pesto

Baba Ganoush (page 36)

Makes about 20

Cook the potatoes in boiling salted water until tender. Drain, then leave in the saucepan with a folded napkin on top and the lid on top of that. Set aside for about 3 minutes until fluffy. Cool a little then cut in half lengthways.

Peel any brightly coloured ones, like Purple Congo, or any with damaged skins. Add one of the toppings and serve.

Variation: Bake in a preheated oven at 200°C (400°F) Gas 6 for about 20 minutes or until tender. Remove from the oven, let cool for 1–2 minutes, then cut a cross in the top and press the sides together with your fingers. The cross will open into a frothy flower, which can then be topped with your choice of fillings.

Spanish Potato Tortilla

One of the simplest and most satisfying Spanish tapas. If you want to serve more people, make several separate tortillas, don't just increase the quantity of ingredients.

750 g potatoes

350 ml olive oil

salt

6 eggs

2 red peppers, peeled, cored, deseeded and diced (optional)

Makes 12 Ⓥ

Peel and rinse the potatoes, then cut into 1 cm cubes and pat dry.

Heat the oil in a deep frying pan, then add the potatoes and deep-fry, covered, for about 20–30 minutes, stirring from time to time. The pieces should be softened but not coloured.

Remove from the pan and drain in a colander. Sprinkle with a little salt.

Beat the eggs lightly with a fork. Gently mix in the potatoes and diced pepper, if using.

Pour off the frying oil, then heat a film of fresh oil in the base of the frying pan, add the potato and egg mixture, and shake the pan a couple of times. Cook for 2 minutes or until set.

Cover the pan with a wide lid, then, holding the lid with one hand and the pan with the other, quickly upturn it, then slide the omelette back into the pan. Cook the other side for about 1–2 minutes. Transfer to a large plate and let cool. When cool, cut into 3 cm squares. Serve with cocktail sticks.

Yunnan Spiced Spuds

A blazingly hot snack discovered by a friend of mine in a roadside food stall in South-west China – use mild chilli powder for more timid palates. Use smallish potatoes, about 4 cm long.

4 tablespoons chilli powder

2 tablespoons salt

1 kg small potatoes, unpeeled

peanut oil, for deep-frying

Makes about 12 Ⓥ

Mix the chilli powder and salt on a plate.

Cook the potatoes in boiling salted water until tender. Drain. Hold a potato in a dry cloth and pull off the skin using the back of a knife. As each one is peeled, roll it in the spicy salt mixture, pressing it into the surface (you must do this while the potatoes are still damp). Set aside.

Fill a wok one-third full of oil and heat to 190°C (375°F) or fill and heat a deep-fryer to the manufacturer's recommended level. Add the potatoes in batches and fry for 2–3 minutes, or until golden.

Remove with a slotted spoon, drain, then serve on a plate, or in a bowl or basket.

Char-grilled Asparagus

Char-grilling produces a delicious flavour, but you can also microwave or steam the asparagus, plunge into cold water, then drain and plunge into iced water. Drain and serve. Freshly grated Parmesan cheese, plain sea salt flakes, aioli (page 37), or chilli oil mixed with rice vinegar are all perfect accompaniments.

olive oil, for brushing

1–3 asparagus spears per person

sea salt, for sprinkling

Serves 1 ⓥ

Brush a stove-top grill pan with olive oil, add the asparagus and press them down with a spatula. Cook for 2 minutes on each side (they should be barely cooked), then arrange, tips all one way, on a serving plate.

Alternatively, cook in a microwave for about 2 minutes or in a steamer. Test for doneness (they should be quite firm and crisp), steam or microwave a little longer if necessary, then either serve immediately or plunge into ice water to stop the cooking. Drain, plunge again, then drain and arrange as before.

When cooled, they can be kept, covered with clingfilm, for 1–2 hours before serving.

Fresh Medjool Dates with Goats' Cheese

500 g fresh Medjool dates (about 20)

300 g mild, creamy goats' cheese

Serves 20 Ⓥ

Carefully deseed the dates by placing them on the flat side (press down, if there isn't one), then using a small sharp knife, slit the date along the top. Carefully prise out the stone and press the cavity open.

Cut the cheese into 20 equal parts and carefully press the pieces of cheese into the cavity. Alternatively, if the cheese is very soft and creamy, scoop out 1 teaspoon of cheese per date. Make sure a petal shape of cheese shows through the top of the date.

Cucumber Canapés

According to a vegetarian friend, this is the nicest canapé she's ever eaten.

1 long cucumber, about 4 cm diameter, sliced 5–10 mm thick

a large bunch of mint

sesame oil, to serve

Pea omelette:

180 g shelled fresh green peas

6 eggs

salt and freshly ground black pepper

butter or olive oil, for frying

Makes about 40 Ⓥ

To make the omelette, microwave the peas on HIGH for 2 minutes, or steam for 3 minutes until tender. Beat the eggs in a bowl with salt and pepper and 125 ml water.

Heat a large, heavy-based or non-stick frying pan, add oil or butter and heat for 1–2 minutes. Distribute half the peas evenly over the surface, then quickly pour in half the egg mixture until all the surface is just covered. Cook just until the omelette has set, then slide out onto a large flat plate and let cool. Repeat with the remaining peas and egg mixture.

Slice the omelettes into squares a little smaller than the cucumber rounds (or cut out rounds with the top of a small glass). Arrange the cucumber slices on a serving tray, top each one with a piece of pea omelette, a mint leaf and a drop of sesame oil, then serve.

Savoury toppings and fillings for **toasts, buns, tarts and cones** can be used interchangeably with many of the recipes in this chapter, and with others in this book.

Make life easy! Miniaturized **toasts, bruschetta and smørrebrød** can be finished with store-bought ingredients as well as home-made.

The only thing to remember when making finger food is that the bases should be small and the toppings should stick sensibly, so they don't tumble down people's shirt fronts.
You can serve them in their bread form, but they go stale or soggy very quickly (unless they're Danish, that is).
I think thin baguettes or ciabattas provide perfectly sized toast, but other kinds can be halved, or cut into shapes with biscuit cutters.

Crisp Toasts and Char-grilled Bruschetta

Easy, mini versions of everyone's favourite sandwich base can be topped with ingredients from the list opposite.

1 baguette or 4 small ciabatta loaves, sliced into 1 cm slices

Makes about 30 Ⓥ

To make Crisp Toasts, arrange the baguette slices apart on a baking sheet and cook in a preheated oven at 200°C (400°F) Gas 6 until lightly biscuit coloured. Take care, they can easily overcook – and don't let them become too crisp or they will break when people take a bite.

Remove from the oven and cool on a wire rack. They can be kept in an airtight container for up to 1 week. When ready to serve, crisp them again in the oven for a few minutes.

To make Char-grilled Bruschetta, put the sliced ciabatta or baguette on a stove-top grill pan or barbecue and cook until toasted and lined.

Onion Marmalade

A delicious way with onions to use with other ingredients and in lots of ways – on pizzas, in tarts, on hot dogs and hamburgers or in leaf scoops.

1 kg onions, preferably red, halved and very finely sliced

125 ml olive oil

1 bay leaf

1 tablespoon sugar

a pinch of salt

1 tablespoon red wine vinegar

1 tablespoon crème de cassis

¼ teaspoon ground allspice (optional)

Makes 500 ml Ⓥ

Put the onions, oil, bay leaf and sugar in a wide, heavy-based frying pan over a moderate heat. Cover and simmer over a low heat for about 15 minutes until the onions begin to soften (a pinch of salt will help the process). Stir every few minutes. Remove the lid, add the vinegar, crème de cassis and allspice, if using. Cook, stirring, until the onions have become translucent, about 15 minutes more. Remove, cool and transfer to a lidded container until ready to use. The marmalade will keep in the refrigerator for 1–2 days.

Bruschetta Toppings

Choose from the list on page 58, plus other toppings from an Italian delicatessen, such as:

- finely sliced Parma ham
- Parmesan shavings
- caperberries
- salted anchovies
- cherry tomatoes, halved,

Danish Smørrebrød
(Open Sandwiches)

I include these because I'm Danish, and because the Danes thought of these long before anyone decided bruschetta was the best thing to do with sliced bread. The only thing to remember is you need great bread, good-quality butter and the freshest toppings. Traditionally, smørrebrød are made with halved, rectangular slices of rye bread – but if you cut them in half again, the little squares will make more manageable finger food.

1 square loaf light rye bread (crusts removed if you like), then sliced

lightly salted butter, for spreading

Toppings such as:

leverpostej, beetroot (opposite) and parsley

tiny shrimp, lemon zest and dill sprigs

smoked or poached salmon, crème fraîche and chopped dill

pickled herring, baby lettuce and crumbled hard-boiled egg

smoked ham, blue cheese and chives

Makes about 48

Spread the bread lightly with butter. Cut each slice of bread in half to make rectangles and in half again to form squares. Pile toppings of your choice on the bread and serve as soon as possible. (The butter will stop the toppings making the bread soggy for a while, but don't wait around!)

Leverpostej (pâté)

Leverpostej (liver pâté) is a favourite in our family. When we moved to Australia, my mother tried to buy the traditional pig's liver. The butcher refused (not fit food for humans!) and made us have lamb's liver. He was right – even Danes like this Aussie version.

500 g well-trimmed lamb's liver, skinned, thickly sliced then chopped

250 g rindless fatty bacon, finely chopped

1 egg

1 teaspoon salt

2 teaspoons freshly ground black pepper

2 teaspoons allspice (level)

2 anchovy fillets, mashed with a fork

1 tablespoon butter

1 tablespoon flour

250 ml milk

2 large brown onions, finely chopped

Makes about 1 kg

Mince the liver and bacon separately in a food processor. Mix with the egg, salt, pepper, allspice and anchovies. Chill.

Meanwhile, melt the butter in a saucepan, stir in the flour and cook for 1 minute. Gradually stir in the milk and cook until thickened. Cool, then stir in the onion. Mix with the liver mixture.

Transfer to a large terrine, cover with foil and a lid, then stand it in a roasting tin. Half-fill the roasting tin with water, then put into a preheated oven at 200°C (400°F) Gas 6. Bake for 20 minutes, then remove the lid and foil and bake uncovered for another 20 minutes. When cooked, the pâté will shrink away from the sides of the terrine. Cool and chill until the next day.

Spiced Beetroot

The perfect accompaniment for *leverpostej* – and good with other party food in this book. Sterilize the jars by washing in a dishwasher and filling while still hot.

1 kg small cooked beetroot (boiled)

1 tablespoon whole cloves

3 cinnamon sticks, broken

300 ml white wine vinegar

150 ml measured sugar

Makes about 3 jars, 600 ml each Ⓥ

Cut off the tops and bottoms of the beetroot and slip off the skins.

Slice the beetroot thinly* and arrange the slices in sterilized preserving jars. Tuck the cloves and cinnamon sticks down the sides.

Put the vinegar,150 ml water and sugar in a small saucepan, bring to the boil and simmer until the sugar has dissolved. Pour into the jars until the beetroot are completely covered (make extra vinegar mixture if necessary – the quantity will depend on the size of your jars). Seal the jars immediately. Use within 7 days.

*Note: if serving as finger food, slice the beetroot finely on a mandoline or with a vegetable peeler.

Mini versions
of bagels,
hot dogs and
hamburgers
are popular
party food.
If you can't
buy the tiny
**bagels,
buns, rolls
and
muffins**
here are
recipes so
you can
cook them
yourself.

Mini Bagel Rolls

450 g unbleached strong white bread flour,
plus extra for dusting

1½ teaspoons salt

15 g fresh yeast or one 7 g sachet easy-
blend dried yeast

125 ml lukewarm milk

1 teaspoon sugar

1 egg, separated

25 g butter, melted

vegetable oil, for greasing

Toppings:

sesame seeds

poppy seeds

several baking sheets, well greased

Makes 64 mini bagels Ⓥ

Mix the flour and salt (and dried yeast,
if using), in a large bowl and make a well
in the centre.

If using fresh yeast, crumble it into a
small bowl. Mix the milk in a bowl with
125 ml lukewarm water, then add
1–2 tablespoons of the mixture to the
yeast and blend until creamy. Add the
sugar and the remaining milk and water,
and stir until the sugar dissolves.

Lightly beat the egg white. Pour the liquid
mixture into the well, then add the melted
butter and egg white and mix thoroughly.
Gradually work in the flour to make a soft
but not sticky dough. If the dough is
too dry, add extra lukewarm water,
1 tablespoon at a time. If too sticky, add
extra flour, 1 tablespoon at a time.

Turn out onto a lightly floured surface
and knead for 10 minutes until soft,
very elastic and smooth. Alternatively,
mix for 5 minutes at low speed in an
electric mixer fitted with dough hooks.
Put the dough in a lightly greased
bowl and turn to coat. Cover with
lightly greased clingfilm or a damp tea
towel and let rise at room temperature
until doubled in size, about 1½ hours.

Knock back the risen dough and cut in
half. Cut each half into quarters, then
each quarter into 8, giving a total of
64 pieces. Cover with oiled clingfilm
to prevent the dough from drying out.

Roll each piece into a thin sausage
shape about 5–6 cm long. Taper the
ends, brush with a little water and
pinch together to form neat rings.

As the rings are made, put them
spaced apart on the prepared baking
sheets, cover and let rise as before
until doubled in size, about 1 hour.

Bring a large saucepan of water to the
boil, then reduce to a simmer. Add the
bagels in batches of 6–9 and poach
for 15 seconds until they puff up.
Remove with a slotted spoon, shake
off the excess moisture and return
them to the baking sheets.

Mix the egg yolk with 1 tablespoon
water and brush over the bagels.
Leave plain or sprinkle with sesame
or poppy seeds.

Bake in a preheated oven at 200°C
(400°F) Gas 6 for 15 minutes, until
puffy and golden. Let cool on a wire
rack. (While the first batch is baking,
poach the next.)

• *Store in an airtight container up to 3 days.*
• *Bag, label and freeze for up to 1 month.*
• *Defrost at room temperature.*
• *Reheat in a hot oven for 5 minutes
before splitting and filling.*

Mini Bagels

If you can buy mini bagel rolls, by all means do so, but if you can't, the recipe opposite will help. This filling is American Jewish – my English Jewish friend prefers either cream cheese or smoked salmon (not both) and insists they're really called 'beigels'.

64 mini bagels (recipe opposite)

350 g cream cheese

about 250 g smoked salmon (lox), cut into small strips, or salmon keta (red caviar)

freshly ground black pepper

Makes 64

Split the bagels and spread with 1 teaspoon cream cheese. Top with a strip of smoked salmon folded into a curl, or a spoonful of keta. Sprinkle with freshly ground black pepper, put the 'lid' back on, arrange on trays and serve.

Alternative toppings (from a good Jewish or European delicatessen) include:
- *schmaltz herring*
- *chopped herring and hard-boiled egg*
- *chopped liver and hard-boiled egg*
- *chopped Spanish onion and hard-boiled egg bound together with schmaltz.*

Hamburger Buns and Hot Dog Rolls

You may be able to buy mini hamburger buns and hot dog rolls, but just in case you can't here's a recipe – the hot dog buns are specially measured to fit the most common mini sausages and frankfurters.

700 g unbleached strong white bread flour

1½ teaspoons sea salt

50 g unsalted butter, chilled and diced

1–2 teaspoons caster sugar

400 ml milk, plus extra for brushing (lukewarm or cooler)

15 g fresh yeast or one 7 g sachet easy-blend dried yeast

1 medium egg, at room temperature, lightly beaten

Hamburger bun toppings, your choice of:

plain flour

sesame seeds

caraway seeds

fennel seeds

poppy seeds

rolled oats

several baking sheets, greased

Makes about 80 rolls Ⓥ

Put the flour and salt (and dried yeast, if using) in a large bowl and rub in the butter with your fingertips to resemble fine crumbs. Stir in the sugar and make a well in the centre.

If using fresh yeast, crumble it into a small jug, add 1–2 tablespoons of the warm milk and mix to a creamy paste. Add the rest of the milk and stir well.

Pour the yeast liquid and the beaten egg into the well. Work in the flour, drawing it in gradually from around the sides of the bowl to make a soft but not sticky dough. If the dough is too dry, add extra lukewarm water, about 1 tablespoon at a time. If too sticky, add extra flour, 1 tablespoon at a time.

Turn out the dough onto a floured surface and knead thoroughly for 10 minutes until smooth, very silky and elastic. Alternatively, work for 5 minutes at medium speed in an electric mixer fitted with dough hooks. Return the dough to the bowl, lightly dusted with flour, and cover with lightly greased clingfilm or a damp tea towel. Let rise at normal room temperature until doubled in size, for about 1½ hours.

Knock back the risen dough, turn out and knead lightly for 2 minutes. Cut the dough in half and use one half to shape hamburger buns and the other to shape hot dog rolls.

Hamburger buns:

Cut the dough into pieces the size of hazelnuts and shape into balls. Place the balls on the prepared baking sheets so they almost touch each other. Cover and let rise as before, until doubled in size, about 30 minutes.

Hot dog rolls:

Cut the dough into pieces the size of hazelnuts and shape into balls. Roll the balls into narrow cylinders, 2.5 cm long, then place on the prepared baking sheet so they almost touch each other. Cover and let rise as before until doubled in size, about 30 minutes.

To bake:

To bake, brush the tops with a little milk and sprinkle with the topping of your choice or leave plain.

Bake in a preheated oven at 200°C (400°F) Gas 6 for 15 minutes until they are well risen, golden and sound hollow when tapped underneath. Return to the oven for a further 5 minutes if necessary. If they brown too fast or too much, cover with foil.

Remove from the oven, cool on a wire rack, then split and fill as described on pages 52–53.

- *Store in an airtight container up to 3 days.*
- *Bag, label and freeze for up to 1 month.*
- *Defrost at room temperature.*
- *Reheat in a hot oven for 5 minutes before splitting and filling.*

Party Mini Dogs

A far cry from the ballpark hot dog – these mini morsels are based on the Danish Pölser, the queen of hot dogs.

20 mini sausages, such as frankfurters, chorizos or merguez

1 tablespoon olive oil (optional)

40 mini hot dog rolls (pages 50–51)

crispy fried onions (optional)

a selection of different mustards, such as German, Dijon, wholegrain and English, and tomato ketchup

Makes 40

To prepare the frankfurters, bring a large saucepan of water to the boil, then remove from the heat. Put all the sausages into the saucepan for about 3 minutes until heated through, then remove with a slotted spoon.

If serving chorizos or similar sausages, heat the oil in a frying pan, add the sausages and fry gently until cooked through. Set aside to keep warm.

Meanwhile, reheat the mini rolls in a preheated oven at 200°C (400°F) Gas 6 for about 5 minutes. Remove and split lengthways along the top, leaving attached along one of the long sides.

To serve, drain the sausages and cut in half lengthways. Into each split roll, insert 1 teaspoon crispy fried onions, if using, and ½ mini sausage. Close the roll, pipe a zig-zag of mustard or tomato ketchup on top of each sausage, then serve.

Mini Hamburgers

40 mini hamburger buns (pages 50–51)

barbecue sauce or chilli sauce

baby salad and herb leaves

10 cherry tomatoes, sliced

4 baby onions, finely sliced

40 baby cornichons (gherkins)

Hamburger patties:

500 g lean beef, finely minced (or half pork and half beef)

4 shallots or small onions, finely chopped

3 garlic cloves, crushed

1 red chilli, deseeded and finely chopped

1 egg, beaten

a pinch of freshly ground nutmeg

4 tablespoons fresh white breadcrumbs

salt and freshly grated black pepper

peanut oil, for frying

Makes 40

Put all the patty ingredients except the oil in a bowl and mix well. Take 1 tablespoon of the mixture and shape into a round, flat patty. Repeat until all the mixture is used.

Heat a film of oil in a heavy-based frying pan until very hot, then add a layer of patties, spaced well apart. Fry for 2–3 minutes, turning half way, until cooked through.

Remove from the pan, drain on crumpled kitchen paper and keep them warm while you cook the remaining patties.

Reheat the buns as in the previous recipe, then split, leaving one side attached if possible. Put a dot of barbecue sauce or chilli sauce into each bun, then a salad leaf, a patty, tomato and onion ring. Put the lid on the bun and secure with a cocktail stick and a mini cornichon.

53

Mini Chilli Corn Muffins with Pancetta, Avocado and Coriander

If you're not a chilli fan, leave them out of this mixture – and you can of course use your favourite fillings instead of the one used here.

200 g yellow cornmeal (maize meal)

200 g plain flour

1 tablespoon baking powder

a pinch of salt

2 large eggs, lightly beaten

300 ml milk

3 tablespoons melted butter, plus extra for greasing

2 fresh red chillies, cored and finely chopped

3 spring onions, white and green, finely sliced

Pancetta, Avocado and Coriander

1 tablespoon olive oil

12 slices finely siced pancetta or streaky bacon, cut crossways into 4 cm pieces

2 large ripe Haas avocados

lemon juice, for brushing

coriander leaves

two deep 12-hole mini muffin tins, greased

Makes about 42

Put the cornmeal, flour, baking powder and salt into a large bowl and mix well. Stir in the eggs, milk, butter, chopped chillies and spring onions, mixing until just combined.

Using a teaspoon, spoon the batter into the prepared muffin tins to about two-thirds full. Bake in a preheated oven at 200°C (400°F) Gas 6 for about 15 minutes until firm and lightly golden. Remove from the oven and transfer to a wire rack to cool.

Grease the muffin tins again, add mixture as before, bake and cool as before. Repeat until all the muffin mixture has been used. Eat warm on the day of baking or store and reheat as listed below.

To prepare the filling, heat the oil in a frying pan, add the pieces of pancetta and fry until crispy. Drain on crumpled kitchen paper.

When ready to serve, split the tops off the muffins, cut the avocado into 1 cm thick slices and then into muffin-sized wedges and brush with lemon juice. If the avocado is very ripe, scoop out the flesh with a teaspoon. Put 1 piece of avocado in each muffin, top with a slice of crispy pancetta and a coriander leaf. Put the tops back on the muffins and serve. If the lids are a bit unstable, spear the whole thing together with a cocktail stick.

To prepare the muffins in advance:
- *Store in an airtight container up to 2 days.*
- *Bag, label and freeze for up to 1 month.*
- *Defrost 20 minutes at room temperature.*
- *Reheat in a hot oven for 5 minutes before splitting and filling.*

Goats' Cheese Butter Filling:

Mix equal quantities of soft goats' cheese and butter, roll into a cylinder about 1 cm in diameter and chill until firm. Slice crossways into discs, then assemble with the pancetta, as in the main recipe.

Cocktail Blini

Blini are the one Russian dish that has migrated around the world to smart restaurants and parties everywhere. They could have been specially designed as finger food in fact – each blin is about 3–4 cm in diameter, a perfect one-bite snack (or two-bite if you're being dainty!) You can buy cocktail blini in many supermarkets and delicatessens, but usually they're not made authentically with buckwheat flour. Be different!

140 g buckwheat flour
or half-and-half with plain flour

1 sachet (7 g) easy-blend dried yeast

1 teaspoon salt

1 egg, separated

1 teaspoon sugar

170 ml lukewarm milk

1 tablespoon butter, for frying

To serve:

crème fraîche or sour cream

small pots of caviar and/or salmon keta

herbs, such as snipped chives and dill sprigs

about 4 pieces smoked salmon, finely sliced

Makes 24

Mix the flour, yeast and salt in a bowl and make a well in the centre. Whisk the egg yolk with the sugar and 170 ml warm water and add to the well. Mix well, then cover with a damp cloth and let rise at room temperature until doubled in size, about 2 hours.

Beat in the milk to make a thick, creamy batter. Cover again and leave for 1 hour until small bubbles appear on the surface.

Beat the egg white to soft peak stage, then fold it into the batter.

Heat a heavy-based frying pan or crêpe pan, and brush with butter. Drop in about 1 teaspoon of batter to make a pancake about 2.5 cm in diameter. Cook until the surface bubbles, about 2–3 minutes, then flip the blin over with a palette knife and cook the second side for about 2 minutes.

Put on a plate in the oven to keep warm while you cook the remaining blini. (Don't put them on top of each other.) Serve warm.

To serve, top with a spoonful of crème fraîche, some chives or dill and a small pile of caviar or keta or a curl of smoked salmon.

• Store in an airtight container for up to 3 days.
• Reheat for 5 minutes in a preheated oven at 200°C (400°F) Gas 6.

Filling and delicious, I think **pizzas and pastry** should form the basis of a party menu.

Home-made Pizza Bases

500 g unbleached strong white bread flour, plus extra for dusting

2 teaspoons salt

15 g fresh yeast, or one 7 g sachet easy-blend dried yeast

1 tablespoon olive oil, plus extra for greasing

5-cm plain biscuit cutter and several baking sheets, well greased

Makes 100 mini pizza bases Ⓥ

Mix the flour and salt (and dried yeast, if using) in a large bowl and make a well in the centre.

If using fresh yeast, crumble it into a small jug, add 2 tablespoons of lukewarm water and blend until creamy. Mix in about 275 ml lukewarm water and pour into the well. Pour in the oil. Gradually work in the flour to form a soft but not sticky dough. If the dough is too dry, add extra lukewarm water, 1 tablespoon at a time. If too sticky, add extra flour, 1 tablespoon at a time.

Turn out onto a lightly floured surface and knead for 10 minutes until the dough is very elastic and smooth. Alternatively, work for 5 minutes at low speed in a mixer fitted with dough hooks. Transfer to a clean bowl dusted with flour, cover with greased clingfilm or a damp cloth and let rise at room temperature until doubled in size – about 1 hour.

Knock back the risen dough, turn out, knead briefly, then roll out to 3 mm thick. Using a 5-cm plain biscuit cutter, stamp out rounds. Put onto well greased baking sheets, spaced apart and with oiled fingers press out each pizza round to 6 cm in diameter.

Add toppings of your choice and bake in a preheated oven at 220°C (425°F) Gas 7 for 10–15 minutes. Serve immediately.

• You can also precook the pizza bases at 220°C (425°F) Gas 7 for 5 minutes, let cool, then store in airtight containers for up to 2 days. Just before serving, top and bake for about 10–15 minutes.
• To freeze, cover and freeze for up to 1 month.
• Defrost at room temperature for about 15 minutes, then add toppings and bake.
• Alternatively, add your choice of topping (excluding cheese), to the uncooked pizzas, bake for 5 minutes, let cool, then freeze.
• Defrost at room temperature for about 15 minutes, then finish baking.

Mini versions of your favourite Italian **pizza** might have been especially designed for partying.

Mini Pizzas

Use half-baked pizza bases from an Italian delicatessen, and cut out mini rounds using a glass or biscuit cutter – or make your own mini bases using the recipe on page 60. The same deli can provide a selection of ready-made toppings, and you can make others.

4 Italian pizza bases, about 25 cm diameter or 28 home-made mini pizza bases (page 56)

olive oil, for brushing

your choice of toppings from the list on this page

several non-stick baking sheets

Makes 28 Ⓥ

If using Italian pizza bases, cut out rounds using the rim of a glass or 4 cm biscuit cutter. Place them apart on baking sheets. Brush with olive oil and add your choice of toppings. Bake in a preheated oven at 200°C (400°F) Gas 6 for about 5 minutes, or until piping hot.

If using cheese toppings, brush the pizza bases with olive oil and bake for about 3 minutes first, then add the cheese toppings and heat through for about 1–2 minutes until softly melted, but not running away.

Variation: Instead of store-bought pizza bases or home-made pizzas, you can use slices of bread, toasted, then cut out with a biscuit cutter or the rim of a glass. I wouldn't use packet pizza mix.

Pizza toppings:

Use a selection of Italian ingredients either home-made or store-bought. Don't use more than 3–4 ingredients on each pizza or the flavours will become too complicated.

- Red pesto brushed over the surface, then topped with a curl of char-grilled yellow pepper and half an oven-dried garlic-spiked tomato (page 31) and sprinkled with fresh thyme leaves. Ⓥ

- Bake the bases for 5 minutes, then top with a thick layer of aubergine purée (Baba Ganoush) (page 36), then sprinkle with toasted pine nuts and cracked black pepper. Ⓥ

- Fontina cheese with anchovy and a dot of red pesto.

- Fontina cheese, pancetta strips and cracked black pepper.

- Char-grilled yellow pepper with roasted baby artichokes. Ⓥ

- Oven-dried Tomatoes (page 31) with olive oil or Fontina and tarragon. Ⓥ

- Char-grilled red pepper with fried fresh sage leaves. Ⓥ

- Anchovies with melted mozzarella and dried oregano.

- Onion Marmalade (page 45) with Oven-dried Tomatoes (page 31) or cracked black pepper and sea salt. Ⓥ

- Sautéed mushrooms with Gruyère, Gorgonzola and mozzarella. Ⓥ

- Flaked fresh tuna with spring onions and capers or caperberries.

- Char-grilled finely sliced aubergine with Oven-dried Tomatoes (page 31) and herbs. Ⓥ

Tart Pastry

This easy, basic pastry recipe can be used to make mini tart shells of many kinds. If you want to make a larger quantity, make multiple batches. Do not simply increase the quantities of ingredients. If you like making pastry by hand, by all means use the traditional method. I don't, because preparing for a party is about minimizing time and effort so the excess can be used to make other dishes – and to have fun!

200 g plain flour

1 teaspoon salt

¼ teaspoon sugar

100 g unsalted butter, chilled and diced

1 egg

1 tablespoon milk

a deep 12-hole mini muffin tin or multiple barquette (boat-shaped) tins

Makes about 34–36 mini tart shells or 18 barquettes Ⓥ

Put the flour, salt and sugar into a food processor and pulse to mix. Add the butter and pulse until the mixture resembles fine crumbs. Put the egg and milk into a small bowl and beat lightly with a fork. Add to the food processor and pulse a few times, then process until the dough forms a ball. Wrap in clingfilm and chill for about 30 minutes or for up to 1 week.

Mini Tart Shells

Knead the chilled pastry briefly to soften, then roll out on a lightly floured work surface to about 5 mm thick. Cut out rounds, using a 5-cm plain or fluted biscuit cutter. Gather the trimmings, re-roll and cut out more rounds. Cover the rounds with clingfilm.

Put 1 round into each of the bases of a mini muffin tin, and press into the corners to thin the pastry around the edges and to push the pastry up the sides of the mould. Prick the base of each pastry case with a fork. (Keep the remaining rounds covered with clingfilm.)

Bake in a preheated oven at 190°C (375°F) Gas 5 for about 15 minutes until lightly golden. Remove from the oven, cool in the tin for a couple of minutes, then transfer to a wire rack to cool. Wipe the muffin tin clean and repeat until all the pastry rounds have been cooked.

Fill with your choice of fillings on pages 62–63 and bake as directed.

- *Use immediately or store in airtight containers for up to 1 week.*
- *To freeze, open freeze in a single layer, then transfer to freezer bags, seal and label and keep frozen for up to 1 month.*
- *To use from frozen, reheat in a preheated oven at 190°C (375°F) Gas 5 for 5 minutes, let cool then fill.*
- *To cook a filling in the tart cases, from frozen, let thaw at room temperature for about 20 minutes, then fill and bake according to your recipe.*

Barquette Shells

Knead the chilled pastry briefly to soften, then roll out on a lightly floured surface to about 3 mm thick. Starting in one corner, put a barquette tin face-down onto the pastry. Using a sharp knife cut round the tin leaving a 1-cm edge of pastry all the way round. Press the pastry cut-out into the tin, trimming the excess neatly. Repeat for the other barquette tins. Gather the trimmings, re-roll and cut out more shells.

Prick the base of each pastry-lined tin with a fork, then chill for 30 minutes.

Cut out pieces of greaseproof paper to fit the tins, press into the tins to cover the pastry, and fill with ceramic baking beans or rice. Stand the tins on a baking sheet and bake blind in a preheated oven at 190°C (375°F) Gas 5 for 15 minutes.

Remove the paper and beans and return to the oven for a further 5–10 minutes until lightly golden. Let cool in the tins for 2–3 minutes, then transfer to a wire rack to cool completely.

Wipe the tins clean and repeat using the remaining pastry.

- *Store and/or freeze, then thaw, fill and bake as in the previous recipe.*

Mini Tarts and Barquettes with Three Fillings

Tiny tart shells filled with all kinds of delicious goodies are perfect party food. You can buy the shells, but if they're difficult to find where you are, bake using the recipe on page 60. The shells are filled with a basic savoury custard, then all sorts of other flavourings added.

62

Don't limit the flavourings to the ones described here. Other ideas include:

- Goats' cheese with oregano
- Mixed chopped fresh herbs with Parmesan
- Char-grilled peppers and black olives
- Smoked salmon with dill
- Cheddar cheese and smoked bacon
- Green peas with ham and fresh mint
- Oven-baked Tomatoes (page 31) with basil sprigs
- Sautéed mushrooms with thyme leaves
- Middle Eastern Lamb and Pine Nuts (page 117)
- Shredded roast chicken, with sweetcorn and chilli
- Prawns and spring onions

36 tart shells or 18 barquettes (page 60)

Basic filling: Ⓥ

1 egg

1 egg yolk

200 ml double cream

Asparagus and Prosciutto:

2 tablespoons corn oil

6 slices prosciutto, sliced crossways

1 onion, finely chopped

50–75 g asparagus tips

50 g freshly grated Parmesan cheese

Leek, Feta and Black Olives: Ⓥ

1 tablespoon butter or corn oil

200 g baby leeks, finely sliced crossways

50 g feta cheese, crumbled

60 g black olives, stoned and halved

Blue Cheese, Pine Nuts and Basil: Ⓥ

40 g pine nuts

60 g blue cheese, such as dolcellate or blue castello, chopped

2–3 sprigs of basil

freshly cracked black pepper

several baking sheets, well greased

Makes 34–36 mini tarts or 18 barquettes

Prepare the tart shells or barquettes. To make the basic filling, beat the egg, egg yolk and cream together.

Asparagus and Prosciutto:

Heat the oil in a frying pan, add the prosciutto and sauté until crisp. Remove and drain on crumpled kitchen paper. Add the onion and stir-fry until softened and golden.

Meanwhile, steam or microwave the asparagus tips for a couple of minutes until *al dente*. Chop into 1 cm pieces.

Divide the onions, asparagus, prosciutto and Parmesan between the tart shells, then pour in the basic filling mixture. Cook in a preheated oven at 180°C (350°F) Gas 4 for 10 minutes or until the custard is set and the tops are golden. Remove from the oven, set aside for 5 minutes to firm the custard, then serve warm.

Leek, Feta and Black Olives:

Heat the butter or oil in a frying pan, add the leeks and fry gently until softened and translucent. Divide the leeks, feta and olives between the tart shells, then pour in the egg mixture. Cook as for Asparagus and Prosciutto and serve warm.

Blue Cheese, Pine Nuts and Basil:

Heat a frying pan, add the pine nuts and stir-fry until golden. Divide the cheese between the tart shells, add the egg mixture, top with pine nuts and bake as before. Serve warm, topped with basil sprigs and pepper.

- *The tartlet shells and barquette shells can be prepared, stored and thawed if necessary as described on page 61.*
- *If you store them, recrisp in a preheated oven at 190°C (375°F) Gas 5 for 5 minutes. Let cool, then fill as above.*
- *The filling, except for the egg mixture, can be added up to 3 hours before baking. Add the egg mixture, then bake as in the main recipe.*

Spicy Mini Shortbreads

Sweet and spicy flavours go very well together. These mini shortbread biscuits are great by themselves, and also good with toppings such as goats' cheese and Onion Marmalade (page 45), cream cheese puréed with stem ginger and its syrup, or a leaf filling from pages 78–81.

175 g unsalted butter, softened

75 g golden caster sugar

a pinch of salt

250 g plain flour, sifted

25 g rice flour, ground rice or cornflour

Chilli Shortbread:

1 teaspoon chilli powder

Ginger Shortbread:

½ teaspoon ground ginger

25 g preserved stem ginger, finely chopped

2 tablespoons ginger syrup from the jar

Spice Shortbread:

2 teaspoons mixed spice

several baking sheets

Makes 100 mini biscuits Ⓥ

Using a wooden spoon or electric whisk, cream the butter and sugar until light and creamy.

If making Chilli Shortbread, add the chilli powder. If making Ginger Shortbread, add the ground and stem ginger and ginger syrup. If making Spice Shortbread, add the mixed spice.

Add the salt, flour and rice flour, ground rice or cornflour and mix to a firm dough.

Alternatively, put all the ingredients into a food processor and mix until the shortbread dough comes together. Wrap in clingfilm and let chill for 1 hour or up to 1 week.

When ready to bake, knead the dough briefly to soften, then roll out on a lightly floured surface to about 5 mm thick. Using a 3.5-cm fluted or plain biscuit cutter, or the rim of a champagne flute, stamp out rounds. Gather the trimmings and continue rolling and cutting until all the dough has been used.

Put the shortbread rounds, spaced slightly apart, on the prepared baking sheets and bake in a preheated oven at 180°C (350°F) Gas 4 for about 12 minutes until just golden. Let cool for about 3 minutes then transfer to a wire rack to cool completely.

- *The cooled shortbread can be stored in an airtight container for up to 1 week.*
- *To freeze, place the uncooked shortbread rounds layered between sheets of greaseproof paper. Freeze, transfer to freezer bags, seal, label and keep frozen for up to 1 month.*
- *The uncooked dough can also be frozen for up to 1 month. Thaw in the refrigerator overnight before kneading and rolling.*
- *To bake from frozen, transfer the frozen rounds to greased baking sheets and bake at 180°C (350°F) Gas 4 for 12–15 minutes or until just golden.*

64

Anchovy Pastry Pinwheels

These simple savoury biscuits are delicious with anchovy, but you can try other variations, such as red pesto or Gentlemen's Relish.

50 g canned anchovy fillets, finely chopped

500 g puff pastry, either fresh ready-made or frozen and thawed

beaten egg, to seal

several damp, non-stick baking sheets

Makes about 60

Put the anchovies in a mortar and pestle, add 1 teaspoon water and mash or grind to a paste. Keep adding water until a smooth brushable liquid results.

Roll out the pastry on a floured work surface to 5 mm thick.

Using a pastry brush, brush the anchovy mixture all over the surface (not too thick, or the taste will be too strong).

Brush the far edge with beaten egg.

Starting at the edge nearest you, roll up the pastry into a sausage shape about 3 cm thick, and press the egg-washed edge to seal. Chill for 30 minutes.

Cut the sausage crossways into 5-mm thick slices and arrange apart on damp, non-stick baking sheets (sprinkle it with water if necessary).

Bake, in batches if necessary, in a preheated oven at 200°C (400°F) Gas 6 for about 10–12 minutes until crisp and golden. Remove from the oven, let cool for about 3 minutes, then transfer to a wire rack to cool completely.

• The cooled pinwheels can be stored in an airtight container for up to 3 days.

Spice-speckled Cheese Straws

Home-made cheese straws taste better than the bought variety, and are very easy to make.

150 g plain flour

½ teaspoon salt

1 teaspoon dry mustard

50 g cheddar cheese, grated

2 tablespoons freshly grated Parmesan cheese

60 g butter, chilled and diced

1 egg yolk

juice of ½ lemon

paprika, for dusting (optional)

several baking sheets, greased

Makes 36 Ⓥ

Put the flour, salt, mustard and cheeses in a food processor and pulse to mix. Add the butter and pulse until the mixture resembles fine breadcrumbs.

Mix the egg yolk and lemon juice in a small jug, then pour into the processor with the motor running. Stop mixing when the mixture forms a ball, then transfer to a floured surface and knead briefly to form a ball.

Roll out the dough to a rectangle 5 mm thick. Using a hot, sharp knife, cut into strips 1 cm wide and 7 cm long. Twist into spirals and place apart on baking sheets.

Bake in a preheated oven at 180°C (350°F) Gas 4 for about 10 minutes until golden. Remove from the oven, dust with paprika if using, then cool on the baking sheet.

• *The cooled straws can be stored in an airtight container for up to 3 days.*

67

Variation:
An easy version is to roll out store-bought
puff pastry until very thin, sprinkle with
freshly grated Parmesan cheese and
mustard seeds, then fold over and roll again.
Fold over loosely and cut into strips. Twist
the strips into spirals and place apart on a
greased baking sheet. Press the ends down
and bake as in the main recipe.

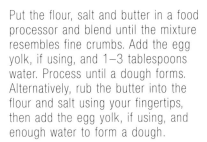

Shortcrust Pastry Cones

Make pastry cones using cream horn moulds. You can start from scratch with this home-made pastry, or use 250 g bought fresh pastry. If you use pastry that has been frozen then thawed, remember that you cannot refreeze it in its uncooked state.

175 g plain flour, plus extra for dusting

a pinch of salt

75 g unsalted butter, diced and chilled

1 egg yolk (optional)

milk, for brushing

1 egg yolk, beaten with a little cold milk, to glaze

12 cream horn moulds and 1 baking sheet, greased with butter

Makes 24 pastry cones Ⓥ

Put the flour, salt and butter in a food processor and blend until the mixture resembles fine crumbs. Add the egg yolk, if using, and 1–3 tablespoons water. Process until a dough forms. Alternatively, rub the butter into the flour and salt using your fingertips, then add the egg yolk, if using, and enough water to form a dough.

On a lightly floured work surface, roll out the pastry into a 35 x 25 cm rectangle and trim the edges to neaten. Using a sharp knife or a pastry wheel, cut the pastry lengthways into 24 strips, 1 cm wide.

Brush one side of each pastry strip with milk to moisten and wind the strips around the moulds, starting at the narrow tip of each mould, overlapping the pastry slightly by 3 mm and finishing neatly on the underside (the pastry should not overlap the metal rim of the mould). Put the pastry-wrapped moulds on the baking sheets so the join is underneath. Brush with the beaten egg and milk mixture to glaze.

Bake in 2 batches of 12 in a preheated oven at 190°C (375°F) Gas 5 for 15–20 minutes until golden. Cool for a few minutes, then carefully twist the pastry cones away from the moulds and let them cool completely on a wire rack.

• *Thoroughly cooled cones can be stored in airtight containers for up to 3 days.*
• *Alternatively, freeze in a single layer, then transfer to freezer bags, seal, label and keep frozen for up to 1 month.*
• *Thaw at normal room temperature for 20 minutes.*
• *Recrisp in a preheated oven at 190°C (375°F) Gas 5 for 5 minutes. Let cool, then fill as in the main recipe.*

Pea and Potato Curry

Use these pastry cones to serve your favourite savoury mixture. Mine is this Indian vegetarian curry – also used for the samosa filling on page 86.

500 g potatoes

250 g carrots, peeled and diced

100 g shelled peas, fresh or frozen

2 tablespoons corn or sunflower oil

2 onions, sliced

2 tomatoes, chopped

3 red chillies, deseeded and finely chopped

1 teaspoon ground cumin

1 teaspoon ground turmeric

a pinch of salt

Makes about 750 ml Ⓥ

Cook the potatoes whole in boiling salted water until half-cooked. Remove with a slotted spoon, add the carrots and fresh peas, if using, and part-cook them in the same way. Drain. Holding the potatoes in a cloth, pull off the skins and dice the flesh.

Heat the oil in a frying pan, add the onions and fry until softened and translucent. Add the potatoes and fry until lightly golden. Add the tomatoes, chillies, cumin, turmeric and salt and stir-fry for 2 minutes. Add the part-cooked or frozen peas and carrots and stir-fry until tender.* Spoon into cones and serve.

*Note: The curry can be prepared to this point, cooled and reheated before serving. Potato curries do not freeze successfully, but this one tastes even better when prepared the day before and reheated.

69

Perfect with finger food,
leaves and seaweed
add crunch and flavour as
well as natural wrapability to
other savoury ingredients.

Everyone loves **sushi** and the home-made kind tastes much more delicious than the shop-bought variety. It's also very easy to make.

The major requirement is the right kind of rice — aromatic, Japanese sushi rice that sticks together inside the seaweed.

Sushi rice is sold in large supermarkets, specialist food stores and Asian markets, which also sell special sushi fillings.

For rolling, use a sushi mat (sold in many supermarkets) or an ordinary bamboo placemat. (Rice should always be measured by volume, not weight.)

Sushi Rice

500 ml sushi rice

Sushi vinegar:

140 ml Japanese rice vinegar

5 tablespoons sugar

4 teaspoons sea salt

6 cm fresh ginger, grated, then squeezed in a garlic crusher

3 garlic cloves, crushed

Makes 2 sushi rolls, 6 slices each Ⓥ

Wash the rice 5 times in cold water. Let drain in a wire sieve for at least 30 minutes, or overnight.

Put in a saucepan with 580 ml (the same volume of water plus 15 per cent more). Cover tightly, bring to the boil over a high heat. Reduce the heat to medium and boil for 10 minutes. Reduce the heat to low and simmer for 5 minutes. **Do not raise the lid.**

Still covered, let rest for 10 minutes.

Mix the vinegar, sugar, salt, ginger and garlic in a saucepan over low heat.

Spread the rice over a wide dish, cut through with a rice paddle or wooden spoon, and fan a little to cool. Cut the vinegar mixture through the rice with the spoon.

Use immediately while still tepid. **Do not chill** – cold spoils sushi and the rice contains vinegar, which will preserve it for a short time.

The rice is now ready to be assembled in any one of the following ways. For a party, prepare at least 3 kinds, with one of each kind per person.

Variation: Add 1 sheet of kombu seaweed, wiped with a cloth, then slashed several times with a knife, to the rice cooking water. Bring slowly to the boil, then discard the seaweed just before the water reaches boiling point.

Cucumber Sushi

This simple, traditional sushi is a favourite with vegetarians.

1 sheet nori seaweed, toasted

1 quantity sushi rice (see opposite)

½ teaspoon wasabi paste

1 mini cucumber, deseeded and sliced lengthways

Makes 12 Ⓥ

Cut the seaweed in half. Put one piece on a bamboo sushi mat, shiny side down. Divide the rice in 2* and press each portion into a cylinder shape. Put one of the cylinders in the middle of one piece of seaweed and press out the rice to meet the front edge. Press towards the far edge, leaving about 1–2 cm bare.

Brush ¼ teaspoon wasabi down the middle of the rice and put a line of cucumber on top.

Roll the mat gently starting from the front edge, pinch together, then complete the roll and squeeze firmly. Make a second cylinder using the remaining ingredients.

The sushi can be wrapped in clingflim and left like this until you are ready to cut and serve.

To serve, cut in half with a wet knife and trim off the end (optional – you may like to leave a 'cockade' of cucumber sticking out the end). Cut each half in 3 and arrange on a serving platter. Small dishes of Japanese tamari soy sauce, pink pickled ginger and wasabi paste are traditional accompaniments.

Note: Sushi rice can be very sticky. To make it easier to handle, the Japanese use 'hand vinegar' – a bowl of water with a splash of vinegar added.

73

Sushi Allsorts:
Fillings and Toppings

Use your choice of 1–5 of the ingredients listed below and arrange them in a line across the rice 3 cm from the front edge. If using more than 2 fillings, use a whole sheet of seaweed instead of half. The roll is completed and cut as in the main recipe.

- Spring onions, finely sliced lengthways
- Carrots, finely sliced then blanched
- Daikon (mooli), finely sliced lengthways
- Cucumber, deseeded and sliced lengthways
- Green beans or snake beans, blanched
- Red and/or yellow peppers, cored, deseeded and sliced into strips
- Trout or salmon caviar
- Smoked fish, cut into long shreds
- Very fresh fish fillets, sliced and marinated in lime juice or rice vinegar for 30 minutes
- Cooked prawns, peeled, deveined and halved lengthways
- Raw or char-grilled tuna, finely sliced
- 3 eggs, beaten, cooked as a very thin omelette, then finely sliced
- Baby spinach leaves, blanched
- Avocado, finely sliced lengthways

Sushi Accompaniments:
- Soy sauce
- Pink pickled ginger
- Wasabi paste.

Seafood Sushi

2 sheets nori seaweed, toasted

1 quantity cooked sushi rice (page 72)

Toppings such as:
smoked salmon, salmon or trout caviar, cooked seafood or fresh raw fish

Makes 12

Make 2 sushi rolls as in the previous recipe, using whole sheets of seaweed rather than halves. Do not add filling. When the rolls are made, pat them into rectangular cylinders. Cut each one into 6 and pat into tidy rectangles. Top each one with a spoonful of keta (salmon caviar) or pieces of seafood or fish cut to size.

Sushi Cones

4 sheets nori seaweed, halved (10 x 17 cm) and toasted

2 quantities cooked sushi rice (page 72)

Fillings such as:
enoki mushrooms, raw or smoked salmon, blanched asparagus, finely sliced carrot, cucumber strips, thin omelette, sliced, sesame seeds, wasabi and pickled ginger

Makes 8

Put a sheet of nori, shiny side down, on a work surface. Put 1 tablespoon rice on the left edge. Using wet hands, spread it lightly to cover one half of the seaweed completely. Add your choice of filling ingredients diagonally across the rice, letting them overlap the top left corner.

To roll the cones, put one finger in the middle of the bottom edge, then roll up the cone from the bottom left, using your finger as the axis of the turn. As each cone is made, put it on a serving platter with the join down.

Stuffed Vine Leaves

I must admit, stuffed vine leaves weren't my favourite thing – until I made my own. If you have vegetarians among your guests, they will adore these leaves. If you're including rice in your stuffing ingredients, make sure it's well seasoned.

36 preserved vine leaves (1–2 packs), plus extra for lining the pan

olive oil, for brushing

1–2 lemons, sliced

boiling vegetable or chicken stock, to cover (see method)

Filling:

250 ml basmati rice

3 tablespoons olive oil

2 onions, finely chopped

3 garlic cloves, crushed

125 g pine nuts

2 tablespoons dried mint or 4 tablespoons finely chopped fresh dill

½ teaspoon allspice

½ teaspoon ground cinnamon

4 tablespoons finely chopped parsley

3 tomatoes, peeled, deseeded and diced

1 teaspoon sugar

salt and freshly ground black pepper

Makes 36 Ⓥ

To make the filling, soak the rice in water to cover for about 30 minutes. Drain.

Heat the oil in a frying pan, add the onions and garlic and cook until golden. Add the pine nuts and cook until lightly browned, about 2–3 minutes. Stir in the rice, then add 500 ml water, the salt, pepper, dried mint, if using, allspice and cinnamon. Stir, bring to the boil, then cover tightly, reduce the heat and simmer gently, without lifting the lid, for 20 minutes.

Remove from the heat – the rice should be perfectly cooked and fluffy. Add the dill, if using, parsley, tomatoes and sugar. Cool, cover and chill until ready to use, but no more than 2 days.

Soak the vine leaves in cold water for 15 minutes – after 10 minutes, change the water and begin to unfold the leaves, still in the water. Drain. Bring a large saucepan of water to the boil, add the leaves and blanch for 2–3 minutes. Drain, rinse, drain and pat dry with kitchen paper.

Put the leaves, shiny side down, on a work surface. Put 1–1½ teaspoons of the filling at the stalk end of the leaf. Fold the stalk end once over the filling, then fold in the 2 sides like an envelope. Roll up loosely into a cylinder, finishing with the seam underneath. Pat into an even shape.

Put half the remaining leaves over the base of a large, heavy-based saucepan. Add the stuffed vine leaves, packing them closely together. Add a layer of lemon slices, then another layer of leaves. Put a heatproof plate on top. Cover with boiling stock, add salt to taste and bring to the boil. Cover, reduce the heat and simmer for 35 minutes. Let stand, covered, for another 10 minutes, then let cool and brush with olive oil. Serve warm or cool, but not cold.

Though it's not traditional to serve them with a dip, I like them with a spicy Middle-Eastern sauce or hoummus sprinkled with chilli and parsley.

Variation: The lamb and pine nut filling on page 117 is equally delicious.

76

Endive and
mini lettuce
leaves make
perfect bite-
sized edible
spoons.

Thai Crab Salad in Endive Leaves

2 red chillies, cored, deseeded and
finely chopped

1 garlic clove, crushed

5 cm lemongrass, very finely chopped

grated zest and juice of 1 lime

1 tablespoon fish sauce

125 ml canned coconut milk

1 teaspoon sugar

1 small onion or shallot, finely chopped,
or 2 spring onions, finely sliced

500 g cooked crabmeat or shelled, deveined
prawns, finely chopped

a bunch of basil, preferably Asian basil, torn

a bunch of coriander leaves, torn,
plus extra to serve

salt, to taste

endive leaves, preferably red, or mini Little
Gem lettuce leaves, to serve

Makes about 24 filled leaves

Put 1 chopped chilli, the garlic,
lemongrass, lime zest and juice, fish
sauce, coconut milk and sugar in a bowl
and mix well until the sugar dissolves.
Stir in the onion, shallot or spring onion.
Taste and adjust the seasoning.

Fold in the crabmeat or chopped prawns
and herbs, then pile about 1 tablespoon
in the base of endive leaves or lettuce
leaves. Serve topped with finely chopped
chilli and torn coriander leaves.

Hoummus Salad in Crisp Leaves

1 quantity hoummus, home-made or store-bought

4 mini cucumbers or 1 large cucumber, halved, deseeded and finely diced

3 ripe red tomatoes, deseeded and finely diced

1 red Spanish onion, finely chopped

3 tablespoons chopped fresh mint leaves

3 tablespoons fresh coriander leaves

To serve:

24 endive or lettuce leaves

sprigs of coriander

grated zest of 1–2 lemons

Makes about 24 leaves Ⓥ

Put the hoummus in a bowl, then fold in the diced cucumber, tomatoes, chopped onion, mint and coriander leaves.

Put 1 tablespoon in each endive or lettuce leaf, arrange on a platter and serve, topped with a sprig of coriander and grated lemon zest.

Quick, easy and delicious finger food containers, **leaves** can be filled with one of the recipes in this section, others from this book – or use one of your own favourite mixtures. Any good delicatessen will provide lots of other delicious possibilities. Listed here are just a few serving ideas.

80

Leaf Scoop Fillings:

Your choice of:

- Smoked chicken with Mexican Salsa (page 36), shown this page.

- Shredded turkey and cranberry sauce with cress, shown this page.

- Baba Ganoush aubergine purée (page 36) sprinkled with chopped parsley and toasted sesame seeds, shown opposite. Ⓥ

- Soft goats' cheese rolled into balls with a spoonful of salmon or trout caviar, plus pepper and lemon zest, shown opposite.

- Chilli Pork Balls (page 102) with Satay Sauce (page 36).

- Soft goats' cheese mixed with chopped herbs. Ⓥ

- Smoked salmon and crème fraîche.

- Onion and garlic sautéed in butter or olive oil until almost melted, then mixed with ricotta. Ⓥ

- Felafel (page 106) on a bed of hoummus with harissa and mint. Ⓥ

- Quails' eggs or small hens' eggs, halved, on a spoonful of Aioli (page 36) sprinkled with poppy seeds. Ⓥ

- Bocconcini cheeses, halved and topped with red pesto. Ⓥ

- Frikadelle (page 100) with horseradish/wasabi mayonnaise (page 84) and chopped tomato.

- Finely sliced rare Roast Beef with Wasabi Mayonnaise. (page 84)

- Shredded chicken with sweet spicy mango chutney.

- Vietnamese Mini Spring Rolls (page 112) with *Nuóc Cham* (page 37).

Convenient containers for party food, **wraps and pockets** can be used with specially cooked fillings, store-bought goodies, or other recipes in this book.

83

Ciabatta Pockets with Rare Roast Beef, Wasabi Mayonnaise and Baby Salad

These pockets are crisp and delicious. Use ciabatta rolls, halved, or the ends of loaves (use the middles to make bruschetta). Other fillings can also be used, such as the Frikadelle or Chilli Pork Balls on pages 100–103.

1 kg beef fillet, in the piece

2 tablespoons olive oil

12 ciabatta rolls, halved

butter, for spreading (optional)

baby salad leaf mixture

sea salt and freshly ground black pepper

Wasabi Mayonnaise:

1 egg

1 egg yolk

1 garlic clove, crushed

1 tablespoon lemon juice

peanut or sunflower oil (see method)

1 tablespoon wasabi paste or freshly grated horseradish

sea salt

Makes 24

To roast the beef, heat a heavy-based ovenproof frying pan or roasting tin on top of the stove, then add the olive oil and swirl to coat the surface.

Add the whole fillet of beef and fry at a high heat on all sides until well browned – about 5 minutes. Remove from the heat. You can prepare the beef in advance to this point.

Preheat the oven to its highest temperature, but at least 200°C (400°F) Gas 6. Put the beef, still in its pan or tin, into the oven and roast 15–20 minutes. Remove from the oven and set aside to set the juices.

Cool, then cut crossways into 5 mm slices, then into strips suitable for stuffing the rolls. (Thicker will taste better – don't be mean!) Cover with clingfilm.

To make the wasabi mayonnaise, put the egg, egg yolk, garlic, lemon juice and salt in a small blender or food processor and blend until pale. Add the oil, drop by drop at first, then faster, in stages, to form a thick emulsion. If the mixture becomes too thick, add a tablespoon of warm water. Add the wasabi paste or horseradish and pulse to mix.

Cut the ciabatta rolls in half and make a pocket in each half by pressing with your fingers. Add a smear of butter, if using. Put a pinch of salad leaves in the pocket, 1–2 strips of roast beef, then top with a teaspoon of wasabi mayonnaise.

Variations:
• This combination is also good as a topping for Danish Open Sandwiches (page 46).
• Instead of making your own mayonnaise, use best-quality mayonnaise from a French-style delicatessen. Do not use bottled mayo – better to choose another dressing altogether!

Variation:
Tea-smoked Chinese Duck

Rub 4 duck breasts with chilli oil and 5-spice powder. Char-grill on a stove-top grill pan, skin-side down, over high heat, until the skin is crispy, about 3 minutes. Remove to a plate.

Put a double layer of foil in a wok, overlapping the edges. Add ½ cup Chinese tea leaves, 2 tablespoons plain flour, 4–6 whole star anise, 1 tablespoon brown sugar and a curl of fresh orange peel or 6 pieces dried tangerine peel. Put a round smoking rack or cake rack on top, then the duck, skin-side up, on top of that. Cover with more foil, then cover tightly with a lid.

Heat the wok until the smoke rises. Smoke for about 10–15 minutes.

Remove the duck and serve immediately or let cool to room temperature.

When ready to serve, finely slice the duck crossways and serve as in the main recipe with salad leaves and a teaspoon of Chinese sauce such as plum or hoisin.

Note: Tea-smoking is also wonderful for fish such as salmon.

Indian Samosas

Freshly cooked and utterly delicious, vegetarian samosas are sold at roadside stalls and railway stations all over India and Pakistan. A great hit at fashionable parties in Bombay and Delhi, these smaller versions are made with filo rather than traditional pastry, and rolled into triangles rather than cones. Samosas are usually deep-fried, but can also be oven-baked.

2 potatoes, finely diced

1 carrot, finely diced

250 ml peanut oil

1 small onion, chopped

¼ teaspoon nigella (onion seeds) (optional)

50 g corn kernels, fresh or frozen

50 g shelled peas

125 g paneer* or mozzarella cheese

1 tablespoon chopped coriander

2 red chillies, cored, deseeded and chopped

a pinch of chilli powder (optional)

1 teaspoon amchoor (mango powder) or lime juice

½ teaspoon salt

15 sheets ready-made filo pastry

melted butter, for brushing

Makes 30 Ⓥ

*Note: Paneer is sold in some large supermarkets and Asian stores. To make your own, see recipe on page 24.

To make the filling, cook the potatoes and carrots in boiling salted water until just cooked, about 3–5 minutes. Drain.

Heat 3 tablespoons of the oil in a wok or saucepan and stir-fry the onion and nigella until the onions are softened and translucent. Add the potatoes, carrot, corn and peas and stir-fry for 1 minute.

Stir in the cheese, coriander, chillies, chilli powder, if using, amchoor or lime juice and salt. Remove from the heat and let cool.

Unwrap the filo pastry and put 1 sheet on a work surface. Keep the rest covered with a damp cloth while you work. Cut the sheet of pastry in half and brush the sheets all over with melted butter, fold each half into 3, lengthways, buttering between, making 2 long strips.

Put 1 tablespoon filling at one corner of pastry. Fold the corner over to form a triangle. Continue folding until the filling is enclosed and the whole strip of pastry has been used. Repeat until all the pastry and filling have been used.

When all the samosas are made, heat the remaining oil in a wok or saucepan. Add 2–3 samosas at a time and fry until golden, turning them over once.

As each one is cooked, remove and drain on crumpled kitchen paper, then serve hot, warm or cool.

Variation: To bake the samosas, put them, spaced apart, on a lightly greased baking sheet, brush with a mixture of peanut oil and melted butter and bake in a preheated oven at 180°C (350°F) Gas 4 for 15 minutes or until crisp and golden.

To Prepare Ahead:
• Cook the day before, cool and chill. Reheat at 180°C (350°F) Gas 4 for about 10 minutes just before serving.

Empanaditas

India has samosas, England has Cornish pasties, Australia has the meat pie – but Mexico and South America have one of the most delicious of all pastry parcels, the empanada. Empanaditas, the little ones, are perfect as finger food for a party. They are usually made with corn tortilla dough and deep-fried, but to save time, you might like to use ready-rolled puff pastry, then cook them in the oven, as shown in the photograph.

500 g lean minced beef

1 onion, finely chopped

1 tablespoon finely chopped parsley

1 garlic clove, crushed

75 ml dry sherry

250 ml tomato purée

50 g raisins, soaked in water

4 tablespoons slivered almonds, toasted

500 g puff pastry, either fresh ready-made or frozen and thawed

salt and freshly ground black pepper

paprika or mild chilli powder, for dusting (optional)

Mexican Salsa or Chilli Mojo (page 37), to serve

Makes about 40

Heat a non-stick frying pan, add the meat and fry, stirring from time to time, for about 30 minutes, or until browned. Add the onion and garlic, stir-fry for 2 minutes, then add the parsley, salt, pepper, tomato purée, raisins and almonds. Stir-fry until the mixture thickens. Remove from the heat and stir in the sherry. Set aside to develop the flavours.

Roll out the puff pastry to about 5 mm thick, then cut out rounds using an 8-cm pastry cutter. Re-roll and cut the trimmings.

Put 1 tablespoon of filling in each circle, slightly off-centre. Fold the pastry in half and press the edges with a fork to seal. Chill for 30 minutes.

Arrange apart on baking sheets and cook in a preheated oven at 190°C (375°F) Gas 5 for 15–20 minutes until browned.

Sprinkle with paprika or mild chilli powder if using, then serve with a Mexican Salsa or Chilli Mojo.

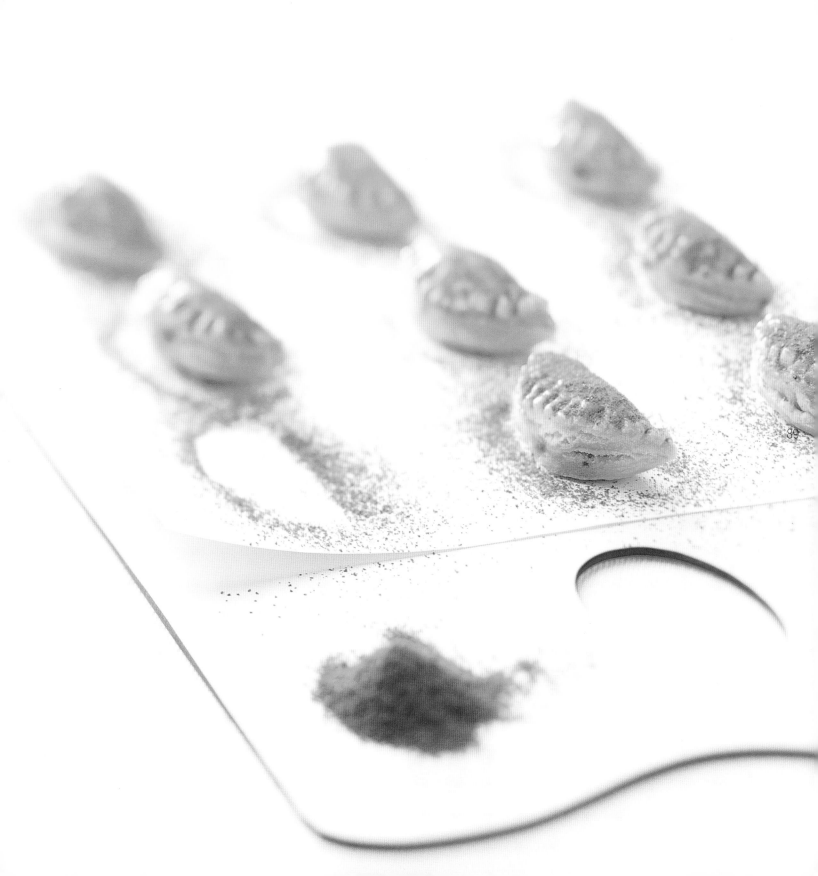

Fresh Vietnamese Spring Rolls

Vietnamese food is full of flavour and not as oily as Chinese. These fresh spring rolls are delicious. They can be made several hours in advance, then sprayed with a mist of water before being covered with clingfilm to stop them drying out. Children love to make them, so enlist their help.

24 small Vietnamese ricepaper wrappers (16 cm)*

30 g cellophane noodles (1 small bundle), soaked in boiling water for 20 minutes, drained, then snipped into 5 cm lengths*

3 carrots, finely sliced into matchstick strips, preferably on a mandoline

1 mini cucumber, halved, deseeded and finely sliced into matchstick strips

6 spring onions, halved then finely sliced lengthways

2 punnets enoki mushrooms

fresh mint leaves

fresh coriander leaves

1 small packet fresh beansprouts, trimmed, rinsed and dried

300 g cooked crab meat, peeled, chopped prawns or stir-fried pork mince

Nước Cham dipping sauce, to serve (page 37)

Makes 24

Assemble all the ingredients on platters and fill a wide bowl with hot water. Work on one roll at a time.

Dip 1 ricepaper sheet in the water for about 30 seconds until softened. Put on a plate (not a board, which will dry out the ricepaper).

Put a small pinch of each ingredient in a line down the middle of the sheet, fold over both sides of the sheet, then roll up like a cigar. (If folding only one side, as shown, let some of the ingredients protrude from the other end.)

Spray with a mist of water and set aside on a plate, covered with a damp cloth, while you prepare the others.

To serve, spray with water again and serve with the dipping sauce – it's better to serve a small quantity at a time, in case they dry out.

If preferred, stir 1 tablespoon sesame oil through the noodles after soaking

Note: The wrappers come in packs of 50 large or 100 small. Wrap leftover wrappers in 2 layers of plastic and seal well. Leftover filling can made into balls or patties, shallow-fried and served with cocktail sticks.

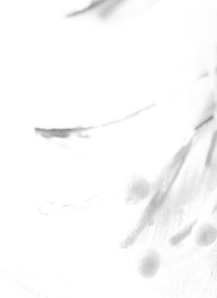

Mini Tortilla Wraps

Tortilla wraps can be made with any number of different filling combinations – just serve your favourites. For a party, however, it's always a good idea to include something for vegetarians – I like avocado.

2 large mild chillies, cored, deseeded and halved lengthways

4 cooked chicken breasts

20 small flour tortillas

2 roasted yellow peppers, sliced

4 Oven-dried Tomatoes (page 31)

1 cos lettuce, finely sliced

250 g ricotta cheese or queso fresco

leaves from 1 large bunch coriander, torn

lime juice, to sprinkle

salt and freshly ground black pepper

Makes 40

Pan-toast or char-grill the chillies until the skin is blistered. Scrape off the skin, then finely slice the chillies.

Pull the chicken breasts apart into long shreds.

Warm the tortillas, one by one, under the grill for about 1 minute until they soften and puff slightly.

Place on a work surface and add a layer of each ingredient in a line about ¼–⅓ from the edge of the tortilla. Sprinkle with lime juice, salt and pepper. Fold over the bottom edge, and one side edge, then roll up into a cylinder. Cut in half crossways, then serve, seam-side down, or tied in a napkin.

Chicken Souvlaki

All the components for this delicious wrap can be assembled in advance, then wrapped and cut just before serving. Roast lamb can be used instead of the chicken if you like. Make sure the chicken or lamb and breads are warm before assembling – and wrap them up in napkins if you like.

4 chicken breasts, skinned and boned, or lamb leg chops, cut into 1-inch steaks across the bone

salt

Marinade:

4 garlic cloves, crushed

1 tablespoon fresh lemon juice

1 teaspoon cumin seeds, toasted in a dry frying pan, then crushed with a mortar and pestle

1 teaspoon freshly ground black pepper

2 tablespoons extra-virgin olive oil

To serve:

1 package soft Middle Eastern flatbread, such as lavash, village bread or pitta

250 g hoummus

125 g tabbouleh salad, store-bought or home-made*

hot pepper sauce (optional)

6 spring onions, cut into strips lengthways, then blanched in boiling water

Serves about 24

Trim the chicken or lamb. Mix the marinade ingredients together in a shallow non-metal dish, then add the chicken or lamb and turn until well covered. Chill for 20 minutes or overnight to develop the flavours.

To cook the chicken, brush a heavy-based frying pan with oil, add the drained chicken breasts and sauté gently on each side until tender, about 15 minutes. To cook the lamb, add the steaks to the pan and cook at a high heat for about 10 minutes on each side until crispy outside and pink inside. Remove from the heat, let rest for 10 minutes, then cut into 5 mm strips. Sprinkle with salt, cover and set aside until ready to assemble (reheat if necessary).

To assemble, cut the flatbreads into pieces about 10 cm square. Heat the pieces briefly, then put a heaped teaspoon of hoummus in the middle, add 1 tablespoon tabbouleh, some sliced chicken or lamb and a dab of hot pepper sauce, if using. Roll up the bread into a square parcel, folding over each end to enclose the filling. Tie up with the strips of spring onion.

*To make your own tabbouleh, soak 125 g toasted buckwheat in water for 20 minutes, then drain. Skin, deseed and chop 2 large ripe tomatoes. Chop a large bunch of parsley and another of mint. Finely chop 3 spring onions. Put them all in a bowl, then toss with 2 tablespoons olive oil, 1 tablespoon lemon juice, a pinch of salt and lots of cracked black pepper. Taste and adjust the seasoning.

Mini Pitta Pockets

Although pitta breads are from the Middle East, the nicest I ever had were in Pakistan – delicious mini half-moons filled with crusty roast lamb, mild red onion rings and tahini sauce. Make these with other kinds of fillings such as chicken, duck, or the Indian Cheese (page 24), or the Afghan Lamb Kebabs (page 122).

24 mini pitta breads, or 12 medium ones, halved

tabbouleh (page 94), salad or parsley sprigs

24 small slices of roasted lamb or chicken, 24 felafel or 24 cubes of cheese, such as paneer or feta

2–3 red onions, finely sliced

about 500 g tahini sauce or hoummus

hot pepper sauce, to taste (optional)

Serves 24

Gently warm the pitta breads and cut in half crossways if large.

Split them open and add a spoonful of tabbouleh, salad or parsley, a few shreds of roast lamb, chicken, felafal or a few onion rings, a spoonful of tahini sauce or hoummus and a drop of hot pepper sauce, if using.

Serve stacked in baskets or folded in tiny cocktail napkins.

A collection of delicious **bites and balls** from around the world. Serve them with cocktail sticks and a dipping sauce — or in pocket breads, on toast, in endive or lettuce leaves, or wrapped in tortillas.

Frikadelle

These delicious meatballs are a traditional dish in Scandinavia, Holland and Germany. Our family recipe includes a seasoning of salted anchovies, which acts a little like fish sauce in South-east Asian cooking – as a seasoning, rather than a flavouring.

75 g mashed potato

250 g beef mince*

125 g minced veal*

125 g minced lamb*

70 g dried breadcrumbs

60 ml single cream

1 egg, beaten

a pinch of freshly grated nutmeg

1 canned anchovy fillet, mashed

a pinch of freshly ground allspice

3 tablespoons butter

1 small onion, finely chopped

2 tablespoons vegetable oil

salt and freshly ground black pepper

rosemary sprigs, for serving

Makes about 30

Note: The traditional meat combination is 250 g each of minced pork and veal.

Put the potato in a bowl with the meat, breadcrumbs, cream, egg, nutmeg, anchovy, allspice, a large pinch of salt and a good grinding of black pepper. Mix well.

Heat 1 tablespoon of the butter in a frying pan, add the onion and sauté until softened and translucent. Stir into the meat mixture.

Wet your hands, take 1 tablespoon of the mixture, roll it between your palms to form a ball, then flatten it slightly. Repeat until all the mixture has been used. Arrange the balls apart on a tray, cover with clingfilm and chill for about 1 hour.

Heat the remaining butter and the oil in a heavy-based frying pan, then fry the meatballs, spaced apart, in batches, until browned on both sides. Shake them from time to time. Remove and drain on crumpled kitchen paper.

Serve with cocktail sticks or rosemary sprigs – the rosemary gives a wonderful fragrance to the frikadelle.

Alternatively, serve with a Chilli Dipping Sauce (page 102), or in hamburger buns (page 50–53), in pitta breads (page 96), as Souvlaki (page 94), in tortilla wraps (page 92), or in ciabatta pockets (page 84) with your choice of salad leaves and sauce.

Vietnamese Pork Balls with Chilli Dipping Sauce

A delicious traditional recipe that's perfect for a drinks party. The original is manna from heaven to the dedicated chilli-head. I am not, and find this amount is plenty. Don't just up the chilli because you love it — remember some people don't. And of course they'll drink more to cool the fires, never realizing that water or alcohol won't help soothe a chilli burn (only milk or yoghurt will, in case you're interested!). Use fat Fresno chillies for a mild flavour, or tiny bird's eye chillies for blinding heat. Fish sauce is used as a seasoning in Vietnamese cooking — like salt or soy sauce. If you can't find it, use salt instead (not as interesting, but OK at a pinch.)

500 g pork mince

6 garlic cloves, crushed

2 stalks lemongrass, finely sliced

1 bunch coriander, finely chopped

2 fresh red chillies, cored and diced

1 tablespoon brown sugar

1 tablespoon fish sauce, such as *nam pla*

1 egg, beaten

salt and freshly ground black pepper

peanut oil, for frying

Chilli dipping sauce:

125 ml white rice vinegar

2–6 small or 1 large red chilli, finely sliced

1 tablespoon fish sauce

1 spring onion, finely sliced (optional)

½–1 tablespoon brown sugar

Makes about 12

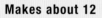

Mix all the ingredients for the chilli dipping sauce in a small bowl, stir to dissolve the sugar, then set aside to develop the flavours.

To make the pork balls, put all the remaining ingredients except the peanut oil in a bowl and mix well. Dip your hands in water, take about 1–2 tablespoons of the mixture, and roll it into a ball. Repeat with the remaining mixture. Put the balls, spaced apart, on a plate as you finish them. Chill for at least 30 minutes.

Fill a wok one-third full of peanut oil and heat to 190°C (375°F) or until a cube of bread browns in 30 seconds. Add the pork balls, 6 at a time, and deep-fry in batches until golden brown. Remove and drain on crumpled kitchen paper, keeping them warm in the oven until all the balls are done. Serve with the chilli dipping sauce.

Thai Crabcakes with Chilli Dipping Sauce

Everyone loves Thai fishcakes and crabcakes. Chopped green beans or chopped asparagus are popular with western chefs, but I prefer snake beans (Chinese long beans) – they have better texture and a more interesting taste.

3 red chillies, cored

3 spring onions, finely sliced

2 garlic cloves, crushed

4 coriander stalks, finely chopped

3 cm fresh ginger or galangal, chopped

6 kaffir lime leaves, finely sliced, or grated zest of 2 limes

1 tablespoon fish sauce

250 g boneless fish fillets, such as cod

250 g crabmeat (fresh, frozen, or canned)

2 snake beans, finely sliced

30 g beanthread (cellophane) noodles (1 small bundle)

1 egg, beaten

2 tablespoons peanut oil, for frying

Chilli dipping sauce:

125 ml white rice vinegar

1 red chilli, finely sliced

1 tablespoon fish sauce, such as *nam pla*

1 spring onion, finely sliced

1 teaspoon brown sugar

Makes about 30

Put the chillies, spring onions, garlic, coriander stalks, ginger or galangal, kaffir lime leaves or lime zest and fish sauce in a food processor and work to a paste. Add the fish and work to a paste. Transfer to a bowl and mix in the crabmeat and beans.

Soak the beanthread noodles in a bowl of hot water for 5 minutes, then drain and scissor-snip into short pieces, about 3 cm long. Mix into the fish and stir in the beaten egg. Wet your hands with water and shape the mixture into flat hamburger-shaped patties of 1–2 tablespoons each.

Heat the oil in a wok or frying pan and swirl to coat the sides. Add the crabcakes, 3 at a time, and sauté until golden. Transfer to a plate lined with crumpled kitchen paper and keep them hot in the oven while you cook the remaining crabcakes.*

Mix the dipping sauce ingredients together in a small bowl and serve with the crabcakes.

*Note: The crabcakes can also be deep-fried in a wok about one-third full of oil. The patties can also be sprinkled with rice flour before cooking.

Felafel

This popular Middle Eastern recipe is traditionally made with dried, soaked chickpeas. Some western recipes substitute canned and drained chickpeas, but this will produce very soft felafel, probably too delicate to serve as fingerfood. Felafel are perfect for vegetarian guests – if the carnivores don't scoff them all first.

200 g dried chickpeas or 500 g canned chickpeas, drained

200 g dried broad beans or 500 g frozen broad beans

1 large bunch parsley, chopped

3 tablespoons chopped fresh mint leaves

75 g bulgar wheat, soaked in hot water to cover for 15 minutes

4 garlic cloves, crushed

1 egg

1 teaspoon ground cumin (optional)

1 teaspoon cardamom seeds, freshly crushed, or 1 teaspoon ground coriander

½ teaspoon bicarbonate of soda

salt and freshly ground black pepper

3 spring onions, chopped

1 leek, white only, or 1 onion chopped

1 red pepper, deseeded and chopped

about 4 tablespoons sesame seeds

peanut, corn or sunflower oil, for frying

sprigs of coriander, to serve

Makes about 20 Ⓥ

Soak the dried chickpeas and broad beans overnight in water to cover. Drain.

If using frozen broad beans, let thaw, rinse in cold water and drain.

Put the chickpeas and broad beans into a food processor. Add the parsley, mint, bulgar wheat, garlic, egg, cumin, cardamom or coriander, bicarbonate of soda, salt and pepper. Pulse until coarsely blended. Transfer to a bowl.

Put the spring onions, leek or onion and red pepper in the food processor and pulse briefly until very finely chopped. Tip the bean mixture back into the food processor and pulse to mix. (Work in batches if necessary).

Set aside for 15 minutes, then chill for 30 minutes.

Moisten your hands and pinch off pieces of bean mixture about 2 cm diameter. Shape into balls with your hands. Spread the sesame seeds on a small plate or saucer and roll half the balls in the seeds pressing them into the surface. Leave the other half plain.

Pour 3 cm depth of oil into a large frying pan or wok. Heat to 370°F (190°C) or until a cube of bread browns in 30 seconds. Fry in batches until brown, about 2 minutes, turning after 1 minute.

Drain on crumpled kitchen paper, then serve topped with sprigs of coriander.

107

Serving Variations:
* *Serve with wooden cocktail sticks, and a dip from pages 36–37.*
* *Serve in halved mini pitta breads (page 97) with salad and hoummus.*
* *Serve in mini lettuce leaves with a spoonful of hoummus and a sprig of mint (page 80–81).*

Delicious, bite-sized morsels, **wontons and satays**, make perfect finger food, and many can be prepared ahead, either wholly or in part.

Chinese Purses

This is wonderful party food, adapted from a recipe on loan from a food-writing friend who gives wonderful parties. Get 4 large bamboo steamers from Chinatown (they aren't expensive) and 2 lids. You can serve one set of 2 while the next set is cooking. If you leave a space in the middle of the steaming rack to put the bowl of dipping sauce, you can cook and serve in the same bamboo container. This can look very stylish, especially if you use banana leaves to line the rack (paper will do just as well, but the leaves give a very delicate extra flavour).

300 g minced pork or chicken

50 g shelled prawns (optional)

2 slices smoked streaky bacon, chopped

1 teaspoon crushed Szechuan pepper or freshly ground black pepper

1 egg white

1 teaspoon sesame oil

2 garlic cloves, crushed

3 cm fresh ginger, grated

a pinch of salt

6 spring onions, white and green parts, finely sliced

4 canned water chestnuts, finely diced

4 Chinese long beans or 12 green beans, finely sliced

2 packages small (8 cm) wonton wrappers*

dipping sauce such as soy sauce, chilli sauce or *Nuóc Cham* (page 37), to serve

Makes about 40

Packets vary, but usually contain about 40 large (10 cm) or 70 small (8 cm) wrappers. Leftover wrappers can be frozen.

Put the pork or chicken, prawns, if using, and bacon into a food processor and blend to a purée. Add the pepper, egg white, sesame oil, garlic, ginger and salt and blend again.

Put all the remaining ingredients, except the wonton wrappers and dipping sauce in a bowl, add the meat mixture and mix well. Cover and chill while you prepare the wrappers.

Using a biscuit cutter or scissors, cut the wrappers into circles.

Put 1 tablespoon of the filling in the middle of each circle and spread the mixture almost to the edges. Put the circle on the palm of your hand and cup your hand, pressing down the filling with a spatula: you will achieve an open purse with a pleated top. Tap the base gently on the work surface to make a flat bottom, and neaten the pleated tops with your fingers. Repeat until all the dumplings are made.

Line several layers of a steamer, preferably bamboo, with banana leaves or parchment paper. Put the steamers, in tiers if preferred, into a wok, pour in boiling water to come just below the base of the steamer, cover and steam until done, about 7–10 minutes. Refill the base with boiling water whenever necessary.

Serve the purses, still in the steaming racks, with one or more small dishes of dipping sauce. Put the next batch of steamers on to cook while you serve the first batch of purses.

Vietnamese Mini Spring Rolls

These easy-to-make Vietnamese Spring Rolls are fresher and less oily than Chinese, even though they are deep-fried.

Remember, don't include deep-fried items in your party if your kitchen is close to or part of the party area. The smells of deep-frying are not conducive to attractive party-giving.

You can make the spring rolls in advance, then freeze and deep-fry them from frozen – or deep-fry in advance, then reheat in the oven before serving.

30 g cellophane noodles (1 small bundle)

5 Chinese dried cloud ear mushrooms or fresh button mushrooms, finely diced

250 g minced pork

½ onion, finely chopped

3 garlic cloves, crushed

3 spring onions, finely sliced

125 g crabmeat (fresh, frozen, or canned and drained) or finely chopped prawns

1 package large Vietnamese ricepaper wrappers (50 sheets)*

salt and freshly ground black pepper

peanut or corn oil, for frying

To serve (optional):

mini lettuce leaves, such as Little Gem

grated carrot

sprigs of basil

sprigs of coriander

Nuóc Cham dipping sauce (page 37)

Makes about 40 mini rolls

The wrappers come in packs of 50 large or 100 small. Wrap leftover wrappers in 2 layers of plastic and seal well. Leftover filling can be made into balls or patties, shallow-fried and served with cocktail sticks.

Soak the noodles in hot water for 20 minutes. Drain and snip into short lengths. Soak the dried mushrooms in boiling water to cover for 30 minutes, then drain and chop. Put the noodles, mushrooms, pork, onion, garlic, spring onions, crabmeat, salt and pepper in a food processor and pulse to mix.

Put 4 ricepapers in a bowl of warm water and let soften for 1–2 minutes. Cut each one into 4 segments. Put 1 segment on a work surface, put 1 teaspoon of filling next to the curved edge and pat the filling into a small cylinder. Fold the curved edge over the filling, fold over the two sides like an envelope, then roll up towards the long pointed end. Press to seal. Repeat with all the other wrappers.

Fill a wok one-third full of peanut or corn oil, and heat to 190°C (375°F) or until a piece of noodle fluffs up immediately. Put 5–6 spring rolls into the oil and deep-fry until crisp and golden. Remove and drain on crumpled kitchen. Repeat until all the spring rolls are cooked.

Serve plain, or in baby lettuce leaves with grated carrot, basil and coriander sprigs. *Nuóc cham* (page 37) is the traditional dipping sauce.

Variation: Try the fresh, uncooked Spring Rolls on page 90.

112

Crispy Pork Wontons

These crispy crunchy wontons produce lots of pizzazz for very little effort. Try this pork filling, or substitute other meats such as chicken, or seafood like crab or chopped prawns. Wonton wrappers are enormously versatile. They come in packs of 40 large 10 cm or 70 small 8 cm wrappers, and are sold in the chiller cabinets of Chinese supermarkets. They should be used within 1–2 days of purchase, but can be frozen if you need to keep them longer.

250 minced pork

4 garlic cloves, crushed

4 water chestnuts, chopped

4 spring onions, white and green parts halved lengthways, then sliced crossways

1 package small wonton wrappers

1 egg, beaten with a drop of water

peanut or sunflower oil

salt and freshly ground black pepper

Makes about 40

Put the pork in a bowl with the garlic, water chestnuts, spring onions, salt and pepper and mix well, using your hands or a spoon.

Take the wonton wrappers out of the plastic bag, but keep them covered with a damp cloth or the plastic as you work, because they can dry out quickly.

Put 1 wrapper on the work surface and put about ½ tablespoon of filling in the middle. Brush a circle of beaten egg around the filling. Pull up the sides of the wrapper and twirl or press it together to form a 'waist'. Open out the top of the wrapper to form a frill. Repeat until all the wontons are made.

Fill a wok one-third full of peanut or sunflower oil and heat to 190°C (375°F). To test, drop in a fragment of wonton wrapper – it should fluff up immediately when the oil is the right temperature.

Working in batches, add the wontons 3–4 at a time and deep-fry for a few minutes on each side until brown and crisp. Don't let the oil get too hot, or the pastry will cook before the filling.

As each batch is complete, transfer to a plate covered with crumpled kitchen paper (skim any debris off the oil between batches).

Serve hot, with a dipping sauce from page 37 or plain soy sauce.

• *The wontons can be deep-fried, then cooled and frozen. Reheat from frozen for 15 minutes at 200°C (300°F) Gas 6 before serving.*
• *The wontons can be assembled and frozen before cooking, but if so, make sure the meat has never been frozen before.*
• *They can also be cooked early in the day of the party, then cooled quickly and refrigerated until ready to serve. Reheat in a preheated oven for about 10 minutes at 200°C (400°F) Gas 6.*

114

Middle Eastern Lamb Boats

The filling for these delicious little morsels should be well seasoned, before and after cooking.

1 tablespoon peanut oil or corn oil, plus extra for greasing

1 packet pine nuts, about 75–100 g

400 g minced lamb or beef

1 onion, grated

1 garlic clove, crushed

4 tablespoons chopped fresh parsley

500 g ready-made shortcrust pastry

1 egg, beaten with water, to glaze

sea salt and freshly ground black pepper

To serve (optional):

finely chopped fresh parsley

sea salt flakes

several baking sheets, greased

Makes 150

Heat the oil in a frying pan, add the pine nuts and stir-fry quickly until golden, about 30 seconds.

Put the meat, onion, garlic, parsley, pine nuts, salt and pepper in a bowl and mix well. Set aside.

Roll out the pastry to about 5 mm thick. Using a long ruler and a sharp knife, trim the edges straight, then cut the pastry into long strips about 3 cm wide, then across to make squares. Cover the pastry while you make up the boats.

Brush egg glaze down two opposite sides of the square, then put about ½ teaspoon of filling in the middle of the square. Fold the glazed edges in half, then set it down, open side upward. Widen the opening to show the filling and make a boat shape, then tap the boat on your work surface to flatten the bottom and pinch up the prow and stern to force up the filling.

Put the boats close together in a single layer on greased baking sheets. Bake in a preheated oven at 180°C (350°F) Gas 4 for about 45 minutes or until golden brown and still moist.

Serve immediately, sprinkled with parsley and sea salt flakes, if using.

Sticks and skewers

are an efficient way to serve finger food.

Fish, meat, poultry or vegetables can be threaded onto skewers and served in any number of different ways – each country seems to have its own version of this dish, and just a few are listed here. These are easy to organize for a party, but try not to overdo the concept. One version is perfect, two are delicious – but I wouldn't do more than three for one party. Serve them alone, or with one of the dips from the collection on pages 36–37.

Lemongrass Sticks

The chicken mixture can be cooked on other kinds of skewers, but the lemongrass gives delicious flavour. You can buy ready-made Thai curry pastes, but the recipe given here is especially delicious. The lemongrass infuses the meat with delicate fragrance.

2 tablespoons peanut oil

600 g chicken, minced

250 ml desiccated coconut, soaked for 30 minutes in 250 ml boiling water, then drained

1 large red chilli, cored, deseeded and finely chopped

2 tablespoons brown sugar

grated zest of 1 lime

sea salt and freshly ground black pepper

10–20 lemongrass stalks, either whole or halved lengthways, or satay sticks

Spice paste:

12 Thai shallots or 1 regular shallot, sliced

6 garlic cloves, sliced

2 red chillies, cored, deseeded and sliced

3 cm fresh ginger, peeled and chopped

1 teaspoon turmeric powder

2 teaspoons coriander seeds, crushed

1 teaspoon black peppercorns, crushed

6 almonds, crushed

1 tablespoon fish sauce

2 cloves, crushed

Makes about 20

Put all the spice paste ingredients into a grinder and blend to paste. Heat the oil in a small frying pan add the paste and sauté for about 5 minutes. Cool, then put in a bowl with the chicken, coconut, chopped chillies, sugar, lime zest, salt and pepper. Mix well.

Take 2 tablespoons of the mixture and mould onto the end of the lemongrass stalks or satay skewers. Wrap the ends of the stalks in little squares of foil to stop them burning.

Cook over a barbecue or under the grill until cooked and golden – about 5–10 minutes, then serve.

119

Yakitori

Small versions of yakitori, one of the best-known of all Japanese dishes, can be made for a party. Chicken thighs have better flavour and are always used in this dish. You can buy yakitori sauce – the Japanese variety is of course the best – but it's simple to make your own. Some of the ingredients are only sold in the largest supermarkets or in Asian markets. If you can't find them, there are plenty of other treatments listed here. However, though green peppers are traditional, personally I don't like them and much prefer red or yellow ones, especially the long pointed Italian ones which are so much easier to peel.

10 chicken thighs, bones removed, skin intact, cut into 2 cm cubes

10 spring onions or baby leeks, halved lengthways, then cut into 1 cm lengths

4 fresh shiitake mushrooms or white mushrooms, cut into 1 cm cubes

4 red or yellow peppers, cored, deseeded and cut into 1cm cubes

Japanese 7-spice or crushed black pepper

Yakitori sauce

500 ml soy sauce

250 ml chicken stock

250 ml sake (or vodka)

250 ml mirin (sweetened rice wine)

100 g sugar

Makes about 30

To make the sauce, put all the sauce ingredients in a saucepan, bring to the boil and simmer for 15 minutes – the quantity should be reduced by about one-third. Remove from the heat, let cool, then chill until ready to use (no more than 2 days please). Pour half the mixture into a small dipping bowl and reserve the remainder.

Thread the chicken and vegetables onto the skewers. For a meal, 5 pieces would be threaded onto each skewer. For finger food, I would recommend 1 piece each of chicken, spring onion or leek, mushroom and pepper. Leave a little space between each item on the skewer so they'll cook through.

Cook under a very hot grill, turning frequently, until the juices rise to the surface, then paint with the reserved yakitori sauce and continue cooking, turning and basting until the chicken is done, about 5–10 minutes in all.

Paint once more with the yakitori sauce and serve the skewers on a platter, sprinkled with Japanese 7-spice or black pepper and with the bowl of dipping sauce beside.

Note: I also like yakitori with furikake seasoning – a mixture of toasted sesame seeds, red shiso and nori seaweed, sold in Japanese shops and larger supermarkets.

Tandoori Chicken

This is the best tandoori chicken you'll ever taste, and probably the most authentic. It was taught to me by Manjit Singh, one of the finest chefs in India, from what is probably the world's best Indian restaurant, the Bokhara in Delhi's Maurya Sheraton Hotel. Tandoori dishes, which originate in the beautiful Northwest Frontier provinces, make perfect finger food. They are cooked on skewers, then removed before serving in a restaurant, but you can serve them still on their skewers.

800 g boneless, skinless chicken

butter or oil, for basting

First marination:

2 teaspoons salt

5 cm fresh ginger, peeled and grated

4 garlic cloves, crushed to a paste

2 tablespoons malt or white rice vinegar

Second marination:

3 tablespoons grated mild cheddar (or processed cheese)

1 small egg

4 green chillies, seeded and chopped

1 tablespoon chopped fresh coriander

1 tablespoon cornflour

100 ml single cream

To serve:

freshly squeezed lemon juice

finely chopped parsley or coriander

Makes about 20

Cut the chicken into 3 cm cubes. Pat dry. Put the ingredients for the first marination – the salt, ginger, garlic and vinegar in a bowl and stir well. Add the chicken, turn to coat and set aside for 15 minutes.

Put all the ingredients for the second marination into a small food processor and pulse until well mixed.

Remove the chicken from the first marinade and squeeze gently to remove excess moisture. Put into a clean bowl and add the second marinade. Turn in the marinade and massage it in with your fingers. Set aside for 30 minutes. Soak about 20 wooden skewers in water for 30 minutes, then drain.

Thread 1 chicken piece onto the end of each skewer. Cook for about 8 minutes under a hot grill or in the oven until half-cooked (put a tray on the shelf underneath to collect the drippings). Remove from the oven and set the skewers upright in a bowl for 5 minutes so excess moisture can drain away

Baste with melted butter or oil and return to the grill or oven until done, about 8 minutes more. Remove from the oven or grill, sprinkle with fresh lemon juice and chopped parsley or coriander and serve on a platter.

Afghan Lamb Kebabs

All through Pakistan and Afghanistan, roadside barbecues cook skewers of lamb, chicken, and occasionally beef on long, dangerous-looking, sword-like skewers. They're much less alarming on wooden skewers. Muslim cooks wouldn't use wine in the marinade, but I think it improves the flavour enormously.

1 small leg of lamb

6 tablespoons ginger purée

½ bottle red wine, or to cover

ghee, mustard or olive oil, for brushing

salt and freshly ground black pepper

finely chopped parsley and chilli, to serve

Makes about 40

Get the butcher to cut the leg of lamb into thick slices, about 3 cm thick.

Remove and discard the central bone from each slice, then cut the meat into 3 cm cubes. Put in a bowl, add the ginger and turn until well covered. Add the wine, then marinate in the refrigerator for 1 hour or up to 2 days.

Remove from the marinade and pat dry with kitchen paper. Thread onto metal or soaked wooden skewers, brush with melted ghee or oil and sprinkle with sea salt and freshly ground black pepper.

Cook on a barbecue or under a very hot grill for about 5 minutes on each side, until the meat is crisp and brown outside and still pink inside. Serve sprinkled with finely chopped parsley and chilli.

Singapore Pork Satays

The Chinese food in Singapore is an interesting mixture of traditional Chinese and South-east Asian influences. Serve these satays with a Chinese-style soy sauce dip, or a South-east Asian influenced sauce made with fish sauce or peanuts.

1 kg boneless pork loin

1 tablespoon coriander seeds

½ teaspoon ground turmeric

1 teaspoon salt

1 tablespoon brown sugar

1 stalk lemongrass, finely sliced

5 small shallots, finely chopped

125 ml sunflower or peanut oil

1 cucumber, quartered lengthways, deseeded, and sliced crossways

1 quantity dipping sauce such as soy sauce, Satay Sauce or *Nuóc Cham* (pages 36–37), to serve

Makes 20

Cut the pork into 2 cm slices, then each slice into 2 cm cubes.

Put the coriander seeds into a dry frying pan and heat over a moderate heat until aromatic. Using a mortar and pestle or spice grinder (or clean coffee grinder), crush to a powder. Transfer to a wide shallow bowl, then add the turmeric, salt and sugar.

Put the finely sliced lemongrass and shallots in a spice grinder or blender and work to a paste (add a little water if necessary). Add to the bowl and stir well. Stir in a quarter of the oil.

Add the cubes of meat and turn to coat in the mixture. Cover and set aside to marinate in the refrigerator for 2 hours or overnight. Soak 20 wooden skewers in water for at least 30 minutes, then drain.

Thread 2 pieces of pork onto each soaked wooden skewer and brush with oil. Cool over medium heat on a barbecue or under a grill until cooked. Thread a piece of cucumber onto the end of each skewer and serve with the sauce.

Indonesian Beef Satays

Satay sauce, made with peanuts, is one of Indonesia's best-known contributions to world cuisine. Make these skewers with other meats, such as chicken or pork – even lamb – and serve with the creamy, spicy sauce.

500 g best-quality beef steak

125 ml coconut milk

juice of 2 limes (about 75 ml)

2 fresh red chillies, finely chopped

3 stalks lemongrass, finely chopped

3 garlic cloves, crushed

1 teaspoon ground cumin

2 teaspoons ground coriander

1 teaspoon ground cardamom

2 tablespoons fish sauce or soy sauce

grated kaffir lime zest

1 teaspoon sugar

corn or peanut oil, for brushing

Satay Sauce, to serve (page 36)

Makes about 10

Cut the beef crossways into thin strips, about 5 mm thick and 5 cm long. Mix the coconut milk, lime juice, chilli, lemongrass, garlic, cumin, coriander, cardamom, fish sauce or soy sauce, lime zest and sugar in a bowl. Add the beef strips and stir to coat. Cover and chill for 2 hours or overnight to develop the flavours. Meanwhile, soak 10 bamboo skewers in water for at least 30 minutes, then drain.

Drain the beef, discarding the marinade. Thread the beef in a zig-zag pattern onto the soaked skewers and cook under a hot grill or in a frying pan (brushed with a film of peanut oil) until browned and tender. Serve on a platter with a small bowl of Satay Sauce.

125

To Prepare Ahead:

• All the satays in this chapter can be assembled the day before cooking.

• The assembled satays can also be frozen before cooking (but only if the meat has never been frozen before), then thawed for 2 hours in the refrigerator before cooking as in the main recipe.

Serving **sweet things** will help bring your party to a delicious end — and a party's not a party without lots of wonderful **drinks**. Preferably champagne, of course, but a truly amazing cocktail can't be beaten.

Dry Martini

The finest and best of all cocktails is this, the dryest dry martini. Traditionally served with an olive, I prefer it 'Up with a Twist' (no rocks, with a twist of lemon). Many people prefer martinis made with vodka, so offer an alternative if you like. The classic mixture, by the way, isn't as dry as this — it's one part dry vermouth, to three parts gin.

1 measure best-quality gin

a whisper of dry vermouth

a curl of lemon zest or an olive on a cocktail stick

Serves 1

Stir the gin and vermouth together with ice, then strain into martini glasses.

Note: Traditionally, martinis are 'stirred not shaken', or at least James Bond said they were. Personally, I wonder what's to bruise! Shake away if you like!

Sweet things

signal the end of the party.

128

I find I don't drink any more alcohol after eating something sweet. These few ideas are easy and spectacular, but absolutely nothing beats a large bowl of strawberries or truly fabulous chocolates — if you're into making your own chocolate, this is your chance to show off your skills!

Spiced Fresh Fruit

A favourite way of serving fruit in India. You'd never think that salt and chilli would make fruit taste good, but both spark up the flavour amazingly.

a selection of very ripe fruit, such as green or orange melons, apples, guavas (preferably pink) and small pineapples

salt

chilli powder or crushed chillies

Serves 1–2 pieces per person Ⓥ

If using melons, cut crossways into thirds, then peel and deseed each third and cut into 3-cm segments.

If using guavas, pink or white, peel if preferred, then cut into 8 wedges. Spear the wedges lengthways.

If using pineapples, cut into wedges lengthways, peel and core, then cut into triangular segments and serve in the same way as the melons.

Prepare any other fruits in bite-sized pieces, peeled if necessary.

Spear each piece vertically with a cocktail stick or bamboo skewer. Sprinkle with a mixture of salt and chilli powder or crushed chillies, or offer separately.

Note: Take care if serving fruit such as apples or pears. They turn brown easily, so should be brushed with lemon juice first.

Flavoured Gelato

This easy ice cream is good served in mini brioches, but I also like them in spoons or tiny shot glasses (before the advent of wafer cones, ice cream was served in tiny cone-like glasses). Use vanilla (preferably pods) as a flavouring, or one of the alternatives listed on this page.

500 ml milk

2 vanilla pods, split lengthways or ¼ teaspoon best-quality vanilla essence (optional)

3–4 egg yolks

125 g sugar

250 ml double or whipping cream

Your choice of flavourings such as:

4 tablespoons Strega or Grand Marnier

500 g ripe peaches poached in 125 g sugar, plus water to cover, then skinned, stoned and puréed

1 punnet raspberries or blackberries, either puréed and strained, or crushed with a fork

pulp and seeds of 6 ripe passionfruit

250 ml canned mango purée (Indian is best)

6 pieces of stem ginger, finely chopped, and 6 tablespoons syrup from the jar

Makes about 1.5–2 litres Ⓥ

To make the basic gelato, heat the milk with the vanilla pods or vanilla essence, until just below boiling point. Set aside to infuse for about 15 minutes. Remove the vanilla pods, if using, and scrape out the seeds with the point of a knife. Stir them back into the milk and discard the vanilla pods.

Whisk the egg yolks until creamy, then whisk in 2 tablespoons of the hot milk into the egg yolks, then the remaining milk, a little at a time. Add the sugar and stir until dissolved.

Transfer to a double boiler and cook, stirring, over a gentle heat until the mixture coats the back of a spoon. Alternatively, put into a bowl set over a pan of simmering water (the water must not touch the bowl), and cook in the same way. Do not let boil, or the mixture will curdle.

Remove from the heat, dip the pan into cold water to stop the cooking process, then cool and stir in the cream. Divide the gelato mixture in 2–4 parts, add a different flavouring to each portion, then churn each one separately in an ice cream making machine.

Transfer to freezer-proof boxes, cover and keep in the freezer until ready to serve.

Soften in the refrigerator for about 20 minutes before serving.

Note: A simpler mango ice cream can be made by mixing 250 ml canned mango purée (preferably Indian) with 250 ml whipping cream and about 2–4 tablespoons caster sugar. Stir until the sugar dissolves, then churn. Don't whip the cream first or you'll get little buttery bits in the mixture.

129

Mini Brioches

You may be able to buy mini brioches where you live, but I can't. So this recipe is just in case. Brioche dough is very soft, sticky and slack, so it is far easier to make and handle if you use an electric mixer with a dough hook attached.
This recipe makes lots of little brioches. If you need less than this for your party, make half or a quarter and use the remaining mixture to make breakfast-sized brioches.

375 g strong white bread flour, plus extra for dusting

1½ teaspoons salt

15 g fresh yeast*

2 tablespoons milk, lukewarm

6 eggs

175 g unsalted butter, softened

peanut oil, for greasing the clingfilm

petit fours paper cases and several baking sheets

Makes 84 Ⓥ

*To use easy-blend dried yeast, mix one 7 g sachet with the flour and salt and proceed with the recipe.

Mix the flour and salt in the bowl of an electric mixer. Make a well in the centre.

Crumble the fresh yeast in a small bowl, add the milk and mix until creamy. Lightly beat 5 of the eggs and pour into the well followed by the creamy yeast mixture. Mix to a soft dough, then fit the dough hooks and knead the dough at a low speed until smooth and elastic, about 5–8 minutes. (The dough will be very sticky and slack.)

Cover with lightly greased clingfilm or a damp cloth. Let rise at room temperature until doubled in size, about 1–1½ hours.

Knock back the risen dough, then add the soft butter, 50 g at a time, mixing well before adding more. Continue beating for about 5 minutes until the dough is smooth, elastic and very glossy.

To shape the brioche, cut off one third of the dough and reserve, covered with greased clingfilm.

Pull off pieces of dough the size of a large hazelnut and shape into balls. Put into *petit fours* paper cases set on baking sheets. For the tops, pinch off pieces of the reserved dough, about the size of a raisin and shape into tiny balls. Make a small indentation in the centre of each brioche base and press in the tops. Cover and let rise as before until doubled in size, about 30–45 minutes.

Lightly beat the remaining egg and brush the tops of the brioche to glaze. Bake in a preheated oven at 200°C (400°F) Gas 6 for about 15 minutes until golden brown. Let cool on a wire rack, then split and fill with gelato just before serving.

- Use immediately or store in an airtight container for up to 3 days.
- Freeze in freezerproof polythene for up to 1 month.
- Defrost at normal room temperature for about 15 minutes.
- Reheat in a preheated oven at 180°C (350°F) Gas 4 for 5 minutes.

Gelato in brioche

These sweet icy treats are a
marvellous finish to a summer
party. Buy the ice cream if you
like, but make sure it's a high-
quality. In case you want to make
your own, I give my favourite
recipe on page 129 – with lots
of flavouring variations. Of
course, if you want just the ice
cream, you can hand out mini
cones, or little tubs with wooden
paddle-spoons.

24 mini brioches (see recipe left)

about 250 ml gelato or ice cream

Serves 24 Ⓥ

Cut a lid off each brioche at an angle,
scoop out most of the crumb and
discard or use for another purpose.

Put a heaped spoonful of gelato in the
hole and put the lid on top. Serve
immediately on a chilled glass plate.

Mini Croissants with Mincemeat and Brandy Cream

Mini croissants are now widely available in supermarkets, especially at Christmas, while croissant dough is available in larger supermarkets year-round. You can stuff these with mincemeat in advance, so all you have to do is reheat them and top with brandy cream just before serving. Delicious.

24 mini croissants, cheese or plain*

1 jar (about 500 g) luxury mincemeat

Brandy cream:

250 ml whipping cream

3 tablespoons icing sugar

3 tablespoons brandy or Cognac

Serves 24

To make the brandy cream, whip the cream and sugar together, then whip in the brandy or Cognac.

Cut a lengthways slit in the top of each croissant. Press a teaspoon of mincemeat into the slit. (The dish can be prepared ahead to this point.)

Reheat in a preheated oven at 180°C (350°F) Gas 4 for 5 minutes. Arrange on a serving platter and top each one with a teaspoon of whipped brandy cream.

*Note: If mini croissants aren't available, you can make your own using the canned ready-to-bake kind – 240 g makes 6. You open the can and the dough emerges, ready-cut into 6 triangles for you to roll up and bake yourself. Cut each triangle into 4 smaller triangles (cut off the point, then cut the remaining piece of dough into 3), giving 24 small ones. Roll up from the long edge leaving the point on top. Bake according to the package instructions, usually at 200°C (400°F) Gas 6, but for a shorter time, about 10 minutes, until golden brown.

Mini Christmas Cakes

At Christmas, everyone will have had their fill of Christmas cake. But it's always nice to suggest the season.

1 section of moist Christmas cake, about 20 x 7 x 7 cm deep

1 package fondant icing, about 500 g

Makes about 70 pieces Ⓥ

Cut the sides, top and base off the Christmas cake with a very sharp knife, giving smooth edges. Cut the cake into 2.5 cm strips lengthways. Cut each strip into 2.5 cm strips to make square logs.

Roll out the fondant icing to about 5 mm thick, then, using a sharp knife and a metal ruler, cut out rectangular strips 20 x 12.5 cm wide.

Place one cake 'log' on one of the strips and wrap the icing around it. Press to seal, tap each surface onto the work surface to form sharp corners. Cover with clingfilm and chill in the refrigerator for at least 30 minutes.

Just before serving, cut the 'logs' into 2.5 cm lengths and serve, perhaps with strong espresso coffee.

Mango and Ginger Kir Royale

Kir Royale is cassis with champagne. This party drink is based on that idea, and if you serve it, you won't have to worry about providing anything else. For my mango and ginger vesion, I use canned Indian Alphonso mango purée when I'm outside mango growing country, and huge ripe Bowen mangoes from Queensland when I'm in Australia. If you're using fresh mangoes, you'll have to add a little lemon juice to develop the flavour, and ice to help smash the fibre.

1 jar stem ginger, pieces cut into quarters

500 ml mango purée

4 tablespoons ginger purée or juice*

syrup from the jar of stem ginger

sugar (to taste)

6 bottles chilled champagne (8 glasses per bottle for champagne cocktails)

Makes at least 50 glasses

Thread the quarter pieces of ginger, lengthways, onto the end of a long cocktail stick or bamboo skewer. Arrange them on a plate, ginger ends downward.

Working in batches if necessary, put the mango purée in a blender, add the ginger purée or juice, the syrup from the jar and 250 ml iced water and blend well.

Add sugar to taste. Blend again, then add more iced water until the mixture is the texture of thin cream (if it's too thick it falls to the bottom of the glass).

Arrange champagne flutes on serving trays, then put 1 teaspoon of the mango mixture into each one. Add a small teaspoon of champagne, stir and set aside until your guests arrive. When they do, top up the glasses with champagne (twice, because they bubble like mad), then put a ginger cocktail stick across the top of each one and tell your guests it's a swizzle stick.

Your guests will want more, so have extra mango mixture ready to hand.

*Note: Ginger purée is sold in jars in some supermarkets. To make your own, cut 1 kg fresh ginger into pieces about 5 cm long. Soak in water to cover for about 30 minutes, then peel. Transfer to a blender or spice grinder and work to a purée. You may need to add a little iced water. You can press the juice through a strainer, or freeze the pulp in ice cube trays and use in this and other recipes as needed. You'll need at least 4 cubes for this recipe.

Mint Mojito

Caribbean Mojitos are the coolest of all rum drinks – and I like them made with tequila too! Before serving, strain this drink through a fine-mesh sieve to remove all the pieces of chopped mint (it's the mint juice that gives it such an amazing colour).

125 ml white rum

juice of 2 limes

2 tablespoons sugar syrup or caster sugar

leaves from a large bunch of mint

ice cubes

sparkling mineral water (optional)

mint sprigs and lime zest, to serve

Serves 2

Put the rum, lime juice, sugar or sugar syrup, mint leaves and ice cubes in a blender, zap well, then strain into glasses half-filled with ice.

Serve straight or topped up with sparkling mineral water, with a sprig of mint and a curl of lime zest.

Frozen Margarita

Margaritas, frozen or otherwise, are everybody's favourite drink. I think dipping the rim of the glass in salt is optional, but the slice of lime definitely isn't.

75 ml freshly squeezed lime juice, plus extra for the glass

salt, for the glass

75 ml Triple Sec or Cointreau

125 ml tequila

crushed ice

1 lime, halved and finely sliced lengthways, to serve

Serves 6

Upturn the rim of each glass in a saucer of lime juice, then in a second saucer of salt.

Put the lime juice, Triple Sec or Cointreau and tequila into a blender with crushed ice. Zap until frothy. The sound of the motor will suddenly change as the froth rises above the blades.

Pour into the chilled, salt-rimmed Margarita glasses and serve with a slice of lime.

Strawberry Margarita

The ultimate girly drink!

1 punnet ripe strawberries (about 12)

250 ml tequila

1 tablespoon powdered sugar or caster sugar

juice of 1 lime

1 tablespoon strawberry syrup

crushed ice

Serves 6

Put all the ingredients in a blender with crushed ice. Blend and serve as in the previous recipe.

California Pineapple Tequila

It started in California, but now this is a favourite wherever there's sun and surf.

200 ml fresh pineapple juice

125 ml crushed ice

50 ml golden tequila

Serves 2

Put together in a cocktail shaker, shake and strain over ice cubes.

Swedish Glögg

Glögg is the Scandinavian version of glühwein or mulled wine – I much prefer it.

2 bottles dry red wine (750 ml each)

1 bottle aquavit or vodka

12 cardamom pods, crushed

8 whole cloves

1 orange

3 cm fresh ginger, sliced

1 cinnamon stick

250 g sugar

200 g blanched almonds*

200 g raisins*

cinnamon sticks, for stirring (optional)

Serves about 20

Using a vegetable peeler or canelle knife, remove the peel from the orange in a single curl (do not include any of the bitter white pith).

Put everything except the almonds in a bowl or non-reactive saucepan and set aside overnight (at least 12 hours).

Just before serving, heat to just below boiling point, then remove from the heat and stir in the almonds. Do not let boil or the alcohol will be burned off.

Serve in glass punch cups or tea glasses, with little spoons so people can scoop out the almonds and raisins. Small cinnamon sticks make delicious, scented stirrers.

*Note: If you prefer, omit the almonds and strain out the raisins before serving.

Children's Glögg

Why should children have all the fun? This is wonderful for non-imbibing adults as well.

1 orange

1 litre apple cider (non-alcoholic)

500 ml apple juice

60 g caster sugar

1 cinnamon stick

5 whole cloves

75 g raisins*

Serves 10

Using a canelle knife or vegetable peeler, cut off the orange peel (not the bitter white pith) in a single curl.

Put the orange peel and all the other ingredients in a large non-reactive saucepan. Cover and set aside for 4 hours or overnight.

Just before the party, bring slowly to the boil over a gentle heat, then reduce to low and simmer for 30 minutes. Serve in punch cups or demitasse coffee cups, with some raisins and almonds in each serving.

*Note: the raisins can be strained out before serving if preferred. Traditionally this recipe also contains slivered almonds: I have omitted them because some children are allergic to nuts. If you like, share 75 g between the cups before serving.

Pimms

This traditional English summertime drink is perfect for parties. When borage is in flower, freeze the pretty blue blossoms in ice cubes for out-of-season Pimms drinks. Allow 250 ml per drink, and at least 2 drinks per person – but be prepared for repeat orders!

1 part Pimms

3 parts ginger ale, lemonade or soda

borage flowers

curls of cucumber peel

sliced lemons

sprigs of mint

Serves 1 or a party

Put all the ingredients into a jug of ice, stir and serve.

Ruby Grapefruit with Campari

Wonderful for a summer party – one tall glass per person as a welcoming drink. Campari at this level of dilution isn't very intoxicating, so this is a perfect drink for early in the day.

1 litre ruby grapefruit juice, chilled

125 ml Campari, or to taste

250 ml crushed ice

sprigs of mint, to serve

Serves 8–10

Put the grapefruit juice, Campari and crushed ice in a blender and zap briefly. Half-fill a jug with more crushed ice and pour in the mixture. Cram lots of mint sprigs into the top of the jug, then serve.

Blue Champagne

Spectacularly chic, this is one you should only serve if you want your guests merry in seconds. Serve to the firstcomers – otherwise everyone will want one!

2 teaspoons freshly squeezed lemon juice

½ teaspoon Triple Sec or Cointreau*

½ teaspoon blue curaçao

125 ml vodka

champagne or other sparkling wine

Serves 2

Put ice cubes in a cocktail shaker, then add the lemon juice, Triple Sec or Cointreau, curaçao and vodka.

Shake, then strain into 2 champagne flutes and top up with champagne.

Triple Sec is best, but can be difficult to find. Use any dry orange-flavoured liqueur instead – Cointreau is the most common.

Champagne Cocktail

There are other delicious champagne cocktails, all variations on the popular kir.

1 teaspoon of a liqueur such as Poire William, peach or strawberry liqueur, framboise, Midori, blue curaçao or Galliano and the pulp of 1 passionfruit

alternatively, 4 tablespoons of fruit juice, such as pear, pineapple, peach or apricot

champagne or other sparkling wine

Serves 1

Put 1 teaspoon of liqueur or 4 tablespoons fruit juice in a champagne flute or coupé and top with champagne.

Note: The glass is sometimes decorated with a slice of the fruit concerned.

139

Cranberry Cooler

Cranberry mixed with citrus juice is a marriage made in heaven – the prettiest, cloudy pink. It's great with vodka in a Sea Breeze, but this soft version is irresistible too.

1 litre cranberry juice

1 litre orange juice

ice cubes

sparkling mineral water

twists of orange peel, to serve

Serves 20

Mix the cranberry and orange juices in a jug.

Put the ice in tall glasses, half-fill with the cranberry mixture and stir well. Top up with sparkling mineral water and serve with a twist of orange peel.

Soft Tropical Sangria

A non-alcoholic version of the traditional wine-based sangria with a South American twist. Use any fruit, but include tropicals, like mango, pineapple or starfruit. Don't use any that go 'furry', such as melon, kiwifruit or strawberries. Wonderful for a summer party in the garden.

1 ripe mango, finely sliced

1 lime, finely sliced

1 lemon, finely sliced

½ pineapple, cut lengthways into 6–8 wedges, then finely sliced to form triangles

1 starfruit (carambola), sliced

3 tablespoons caster sugar

2 litres ginger ale, lemonade or orange squash, well chilled

Serves about 12

Put the sliced fruit into a punch bowl. Sprinkle with sugar and set aside for at least 30 minutes. Top with icy ginger ale or lemonade just before serving. Fill wine glasses with ice, add a few pieces of the fruit, then top with the fizzy liquid.

Variation: Peachy Sangria
Put 500 ml peach nectar, mint sprigs and 2 sliced peaches in the bowl and top with ginger ale or lemonade (or champagne).

Rock Shandy

Pretty and delicious. Bitters are high in alcohol, and though it is very much diluted in this drink, it's still there, and should not be served to people who never touch alcohol.

1 litre sparkling mineral water

Angostura bitters, to taste

ice cubes

sprigs of mint, to serve (optional)

Serves about 10

Fill 10 tall glasses with ice cubes, top with chilled sparkling mineral water and a sprig of mint. Add ½ teaspoon Angostura bitters to each glass – do not stir. The pink bitters will gradually sink to the bottom of the glass.

Choose a Menu

Summer Party

Ice-cold Prairie Oysters
Spoonfuls of Spicy Thai Salad
Gazpacho
Flat Beans with Hoummus
Mini Pizzas
Anchovy Pastry Pinwheels
Sushi Allsorts
Leaves with Baba Ganoush and
  Sesame Seeds
Fresh Vietnamese Spring Rolls
Lemongrass Sticks
Spiced Fresh Fruit
Gelati and Sorbets

Christmas Party

Spiced Nuts
Oven-baked Tomatoes
Blini
Bruschettas and Pizzas
Asparagus and Bacon Tartlets
Stuffed Vine Leaves
Turkey and Cranberry Leaf Wraps
Samosas
Tandoori Chicken
Middle Eastern Lamb Boats
Christmas Cakes
Mincemeat Croissants with Brandy
  Cream

Winter Party

Pea Soup with Mint
Quail Eggs with Dipping Sauce
Yunnan Spiced Spuds
Mini Hot Dogs with Mustard
Bruschettas and Pizzas
Spicy Mini Shortbreads
Hoummus Salad in Crisp Leaves
Smoked Chicken and Mexican Salsa in
  Leaf Wrap
Empanaditas
Mincemeat Croissants with Brandy Cream

Celebration Party

Spoonfuls of Caviar
Oysters on Ice
Plunged Shrimp with Chilli Mojo
Chilli Corn Muffins with Goat Cheese and
  Bacon
Seafood Sushi
Leaves with Goat Cheese and Smoked
  Salmon
Chicken Souvlaki
Yakitori
Christmas Cakes (as celebration cake)

Casual Party in the Garden

Fish and Chips
Char-grilled Asparagus
Mini Hamburgers and Hot Dogs
Blue Cheese, Pine Nuts and Basil Tarts
Sushi collection
Roast Beef and Wasabi Mayonnaise in
  Ciabatta
Mini Tortilla Wraps
Indonesian Beef Satays

Wedding Party

Spicy Caribbean Crisps
Baby Potatoes
Danish Open Sandwiches
Mini Bagels
Leek and Feta Tartlets
Sushi Cones
Thai Crab Salad in Endive Leaves
Crispy Pork Wontons
Tandoori Chicken
Christmas Cakes (as wedding cake)

Vegetarian Menu

Sweet Potato Soup
Plantain Crisps
Baby Potatoes with cream cheese and
  chives
Spanish Potato Tortilla
Cucumber Canapés
Bruschetta with Vegetable Toppings
Leek and Feta Tartlets
Potato Curry Cones
Cucumber Sushi
Stuffed Vine Leaves
Gelati in Spoons or Brioche
Christmas Cakes

Any Party, Any Time

Cheese Straws
Caribbean Crisps
Bruschetta and Pizzas
Anchovy Pinwheels
Mini Hot Dogs and Hamburgers
Mini Tartlets with various fillings
Sushi Allsorts
Mini Pitta Pockets
Chinese Purses
Vietnamese Spring Rolls
Lamb Kebabs
Singapore Pork Satays
Mincemeat Croissants with Brandy
  Cream
Gelati in Spoons or Brioche

Index

144